"Christopher Watkin's *Michel Foucault* does us the a double favor. It briefly and carefully outlines the main features and developments of an important twentieth-century thinker, and it brings these into conversation with a Reformed, philosophically adept account of the Bible. Watkin manages to do all this without any 'ventriloquizing,' of either Foucault or Scripture. He allows readers to sympathetically feel the weight of Foucault's concerns about such things as the telling of history, the limits of cultural vision, self-transformation, and, above all, power relations, before turning to an examination of the cross of Christ that simultaneously fulfills and critiques Foucault's ambitious aims. If God is the absolute being whose definitive self-disclosure is the humble self-giving of Jesus Christ, then individuals and communities can find in Christ an objective, normative pattern of life that neither crushes the self nor dominates others. As I reached the end of this book, I was wishing that the great atheist philosopher himself could have read this friendly interaction with his thought."

—**John Dickson**, Author and Historian; Rector,
St. Andrew's Roseville; Founding Scholar , Centre for
Public Christianity; Lecturer, Faculty of Arts and Social
Sciences, University of Sydney

"Michel Foucault is undoubtedly one of the most significant voices in our times. The twin temptation when dealing with him is either to lionize him as a unique prophet who has unmasked the way in which we all abuse power, or to dismiss him as a Nietzschean voice against truth and divine revelation. In the capable hands of Chris Watkin, Foucault does emerge as a helpful guide to how we use and abuse power, yet one who in the end is deeply flawed. Christians may safely benefit from Foucault as a cobelligerent in several areas, including social criticism, while at the same time recognize the chasm between his approach and that of the Reformed Christian worldview. An absolute treasure of a book."

—**William Edgar**, Professor of Apologetics, Westminster Theological Seminary

"For a long time, I have had the conviction that Cornelius Van Til and the Reformed tradition provide a multitude of insights for Christians seeking to come to terms with twentieth-century philosophy. I believed that a response to certain key twentieth-century thinkers informed by Van Til's insights was just what was needed. Christopher Watkin has engaged in such a task—first with his *Jacques Derrida* volume, and now this *Michel Foucault* volume in the Great Thinkers series. Professor Watkin has spent a lot of time studying key Continental philosophers (including Foucault), and he has a good understanding of Reformed thought. Watkin brings these two worlds together in a great book. I hope he keeps writing, and I look forward to other volumes in the Great Thinkers series."

—**Bradley G. Green**, Professor of Theological Studies, Union University

"Christopher Watkin has been a valuable and reliable expositor of modern and postmodern thinking. The present volume on Foucault only adds to the growing list of his accomplishments. Not only is this volume in the Great Thinkers series a stellar addition, but it is engagingly written with ample illustrations that substantiate Foucault's position among the forefront of apologists for postmodernism. Many strengths of Watkin's analysis stand out. He clearly demonstrates how postmodernist epistemology supplants modern thinkers Descartes, Kant, and Hegel. But he also draws comparisons and contrasts with those whom I call the earliest postmodernists, such as Nietzsche and Marx. He also shows why Foucault rejects the concept of worldview despite postmodern similarities with worldview thinking. Perhaps most valuable, as one would expect in this series, Watkin subjects both Foucault's ideas and similar biblical topics to clear analysis. He labors might and main to be fair to Foucault while comparing and contrasting his ideas with and to biblical passages. In so doing, Watkin reveals a distinctly Reformed perspective. Most impressive to me is his analysis of Foucault's distinction between autonomous and heteronomous transformation of the self. With helpful diagrams (which also appear throughout the text), Watkin shows how to avoid drawing a dichotomy between 'autonomous self-transformation' and 'pseudo-autonomous self-transformation.' Drawing on Pauline texts, Watkin proposes instead 'cruciform identity' and the Reformed perspective that retains both human responsibility ('work out your own salvation with fear and trembling') and God's sovereignty ('for it is God who works in you, both to will and to work for his good pleasure'). I highly recommend this text."

—**W. Andrew Hoffecker**, Emeritus Professor of Church History, Reformed Theological Seminary

"Few Christians are familiar with Foucault. Even fewer actually engage (rather than accept or dismiss) his influential theses. That makes Chris Watkin's book essential reading. Sympathetically interpreting Foucault's basic program, Watkin shows how a Christian interpretation of reality is not only true but more persuasive. I highly recommend it."

—**Michael S. Horton**, J. Gresham Machen Professor of Systematic Theology and Apologetics, Westminster Theological Seminary California

"Chris Watkin has written a remarkable book—remarkable for its brevity, concision, accuracy, insight. This short introduction to Michel Foucault sets Foucault in his philosophical and historical context, explains his main ideas and contributions, and shows what we can learn from him. Best of all for a Christian reader, Watkin assesses Foucault's strengths and flaws in the light of Scripture. This is the place to start for readers who want to know more about this massively influential thinker."

—**Peter J. Leithart**, President, Theopolis Institute for Biblical, Liturgical, and Cultural Studies, Birmingham, Alabama

"If you're not familiar with Michel Foucault, you should be. He is one of the most influential figures, if not the most influential figure, in contemporary Western culture. In this volume, Chris Watkin has accomplished what very few have even attempted. He walks us through the development of Foucault's points of view with expert care and clarity. He also compares and contrasts these outlooks with the teachings of the New Testament in ways that challenge followers of Christ to look afresh at some of their most basic commitments.

"As one who has been acquainted with the writings of Foucault, I've been waiting for a volume like this for decades. It is essential for Christian scholars in every discipline. It serves as an effective guide for Christian leaders and laypeople alike, as we seek to address the needs of the church and the unbelieving world today. If you haven't read it, you should—today."

—**Richard L. Pratt Jr.**, President, Third Millennium Ministries

"Foucault's thinking has seeped everywhere. This was brought home to me as I entered my son's room during his first term as an undergraduate to find books by Foucault and about Foucault. He was studying geography. As with Watkin's study on Derrida, the author is an expert guide in coming to grips with what Foucault was (and was not) saying about history, power, and identity. More importantly, he shows us how this hugely influential 'story' and social theory both connect to and are confronted by the Christian 'story' and social theory in its cruciform shape. We desperately need these analyses. The gospel is big enough, true enough, and good enough to take every thought captive for Christ, and Watkin's work is showing us the way. Highly recommended."

—**Dan Strange**, Director, Oak Hill College

"Watkin has done it again! In less than a hundred and fifty pages of text, he has successfully laid out the core concerns—history, power, and identity—of one of the twentieth century's leading postmodern presuppositionalists, Michel Foucault, and put them into constructive dialogue with the way that the apostle Paul treats these same three themes in the opening chapters of 1 Corinthians. This is a brilliant study of how the story, and wisdom, of the cross continues to confront, confound, and turn upside down the wisdom of this world."

—**Kevin J. Vanhoozer**, Research Professor of Systematic Theology, Trinity Evangelical Divinity School

Praise for the Great Thinkers Series

"After a long eclipse, intellectual history is back. We are becoming aware, once again, that ideas have consequences. The importance of P&R Publishing's leadership in this trend cannot be overstated. The series Great Thinkers: Critical Studies of Minds That Shape Us is a tool that I wish I had possessed when I was in college and early in my ministry. The scholars examined in this well-chosen group have shaped our minds and habits more than we know. Though succinct, each volume is rich, and displays a balance between what Christians ought to value and what they ought to reject. This is one of the happiest publishing events in a long time."

—**William Edgar**, Professor of Apologetics, Westminster Theological Seminary

"When I was beginning my studies of theology and philosophy during the 1950s and '60s, I profited enormously from P&R's Modern Thinkers Series. Here were relatively short books on important philosophers and theologians such as Nietzsche, Dewey, Van Til, Barth, and Bultmann, by scholars of Reformed conviction such as Clark, Van Riessen, Ridderbos, Polman, and Zuidema. These books did not merely summarize the work of these thinkers; they were serious critical interactions. Today, P&R is resuming and updating the series, now called Great Thinkers. The new books, on people such as Aquinas, Hume, Nietzsche, Derrida, and Foucault, are written by scholars who are experts on these writers. As before, these books are short—around 100 pages. They set forth accurately the views of the thinkers under consideration, and they enter into constructive dialogue, governed by biblical and Reformed convictions. I look forward to the release of all the books being planned and to the good influence they will have on the next generation of philosophers and theologians."

—**John M. Frame**, Professor of Systematic Theology and
 Philosophy Emeritus, Reformed Theological Seminary,
 Orlando

Michel
FOUCAULT

GREAT THINKERS

A Series

Series Editor
Nathan D. Shannon

Michel
FOUCAULT

Christopher Watkin

P&R
P U B L I S H I N G
P.O. BOX 817 • PHILLIPSBURG • NEW JERSEY 08865-0817

ISBN: 978-1-62995-348-9 (pbk)
ISBN: 978-1-62995-349-6 (ePub)
ISBM: 978-1-62995-350-2 (Mobi)

Printed in the United States of America

Library of Congress Cataloging-in-Publication Data

Names: Watkin, Christopher, author.
Title: Michel Foucault / Christopher Watkin.
Description: Phillipsburg : P&R Publishing, 2018. | Series: Great thinkers: a series | Includes bibliographical references and index.
Identifiers: LCCN 2018007288| ISBN 9781629953489 (pbk.) | ISBN 9781629953496 (epub) | ISBN 9781629953502 (mobi)
Subjects: LCSH: Foucault, Michel, 1926-1984. | Reformed Church--Doctrines.
Classification: LCC B2430.F724 W38 2018 | DDC 194--dc23
LC record available at https://lccn.loc.gov/2018007288

To all those for whom *audi alteram partem*
is a virtue, not a weakness

CONTENTS

SERIES INTRODUCTION

Amid the rise and fall of nations and civilizations, the influence of a few great minds has been profound. Some of these remain relatively obscure, even as their thought shapes our world; others have become household names. As we engage our cultural and social contexts as ambassadors and witnesses for Christ, we must identify and test against the Word those thinkers who have so singularly formed the present age.

The Great Thinkers series is designed to meet the need for critically assessing the seminal thoughts of these thinkers. Great Thinkers hosts a colorful roster of authors analyzing primary source material against a background of historical contextual issues, and providing rich theological assessment and response from a Reformed perspective.

Each author was invited to meet a threefold goal, so that each Great Thinkers volume is, first, *academically informed.* The brevity of Great Thinkers volumes sets a premium on each author's command of the subject matter and on the secondary discussions that have shaped each thinker's influence. Our authors identify the most influential features of their thinkers' work and address them with precision and insight. Second, the series maintains a high standard of *biblical and theological faithfulness*. Each volume stands on an epistemic commitment to "the whole counsel of God" (Acts 20:27), and is thereby equipped for fruitful critical engagement. Finally, Great Thinkers texts are *accessible*, not burdened with jargon or unnecessarily difficult vocabulary. The goal is to inform and equip the reader as effectively as possible through clear writing, relevant analysis, and incisive, constructive critique. My hope is that this series will distinguish itself by striking with biblical faithfulness and the riches of the Reformed tradition at the central nerves of culture, cultural history, and intellectual heritage.

Bryce Craig, president of P&R Publishing, deserves hearty thanks for his initiative and encouragement in setting the series in motion and seeing it through. Many thanks as well to P&R's director of academic development, John Hughes, who has assumed, with cool efficiency, nearly every role on the production side of each volume. The Rev. Mark Moser carried much of the burden in the initial design of the series, acquisitions, and editing of the first several volumes. And the expert participation of Amanda Martin, P&R's editorial director, was essential at every turn. I have long admired P&R Publishing's commitment, steadfast now for over eighty-five years, to publishing excellent books promoting biblical understanding and cultural awareness, especially in the area of Christian apologetics. Sincere thanks to P&R, to these fine brothers and sisters, and to several others not mentioned here for the opportunity to serve as editor of the Great Thinkers series.

Nathan D. Shannon
Seoul, Korea

FOREWORD

It is the task of a foreword to commend a work to you, the reader, and to say why this work matters. I will endeavor to fulfill this task, one that is at once easy and somewhat difficult. It is easy because Christopher Watkin's Foucault is a highly commendable venture; it is difficult because our times, and the common configuration of our Christian practice within them, are disinclined to entertain such ventures.

We live in modernity, in the modern West. Modernism, the prevailing pattern of thought and culture beginning perhaps most obviously in the 1600s and still growing in trenchancy, strongly inclines us to the pragmatic and away from the useless. It deems philosophy and philosophical awareness useless, unpragmatic, and thus suspect. It imagines that it is something that one might opt out of. It blinds its children to the ironically philosophical nature of this claim. Modernism is a philosophical outlook that is compulsively antiphilosophical.

Modern Western Christian practice bears the same marks: we are pragmatic about the gospel and its dissemination. We can be something like the reverse of the emperor in his imagined clothes: we imagine that we are free of philosophical commitments when all the while the child can plainly see that our very selves have been woven into the warp and woof of the philosophical fabric. Such Christians are disinclined even to open such a book as this. Or if we do, it is only to vindicate the Christian religion in rejection of the world.

But you have opened it! Good! Indeed, there should in fact be a deeper reality that is calling you; for there is one thing you need in order to be philosophical, and that is to be born. To be human is to ponder deep questions of wonder—something that dogs, for example, just don't do.

Also, you know that there are Christian doctrines that commend a wider outlook, a profounder grasp of life and thinking. To name a couple here: (1) To love God is also to love his works, and that includes the stuff of reality and our own times. God is Lord; humans are image-bearers. Although human personal and structural sin warps our understanding (case in point: modernism—thus it's worth joining Foucault in combating it), truth happens in every corner of the earth, and where it happens, it is the Lord's. (2) The gospel of Jesus Christ should be the transformative, subversive center of everything, even (especially) our deepest philosophical commitments. David Kettle, following in the missiological vision of Lesslie Newbigin, describes the gospel and conversion as the hospitable approach of God to "break in and break open" our world—what Watkin calls diagonalization and the cruciform reversal.[1] The gospel both honors the world and transforms it, welcoming it into its coming. These Christian truths situate and heighten the import of this little book on Michel Foucault, and the value (nonpragmatic—but pragmatic as well) of the listening to Foucault that it models and commends.

1. David J. Kettle, Western Culture in Gospel Context: Towards the Conversion of the West: Theological Bearings for Mission and Spirituality (Eugene, OR: Cascade Books, 2011).

Foucault, it turns out, voices modernism deeply, helping us to understand it and to humbly notice our own clothes. Give philosophical awareness a chance (philosophical friendship, too!), and you will find that you love it, and love it as loving God and his (also our) world.

Foucault understands and propounds some things about power in modernity: that it is pervasive, internalized, bodied, that it's really helpful to discern and be responsible about the power-knowledge connection, that it may not look like what we moderns have been touting, that our blindness typifies modernism, and that modernism needs to be subverted if we are going to survive.

I am an educator: the impinging world of my work is one of standards, assessments, data, scantrons with a-to-e options, and (most prized) results. No one, it can seem, even sees the actually pretty high-handed power nexus here. Only five options? Whose universe are scantron people in? Sadly, they are in the modernist one. Who determines what those five options are? How is it that we acquiesce blithely to such an anonymous, two-dimensional but commodifiable version of reality and of ourselves as educated?

I now make my home in Aliquippa, Pennsylvania. At one time, Pittsburgh was corporate capital of the world, and Aliquippa was home to the world's largest steel mill, sprawled seven miles along the Ohio River here. The stories of the mills are of vast wealth in exchange for personal bondage and addiction: a self-chosen participation in dangerous work, in which on-the-job deaths and disability were rationalized to be the price of progress.[2] Foucault somewhere argues that capitalism requires the kind of internalized discipline that typifies modernity.

2. I follow John Stanley, formerly of Uncommongrounds Café, a Church Army mission in Aliquippa, in comparing this favorably to Walter Brueggemann's account of the "royal consciousness" ascendant in Israel in Solomon's era, in his Prophetic Imagination, 2nd ed. (Minneapolis: Fortress Press, 2001).

I am a woman. In my admittedly few PowerPoint slides devoted to Foucault in my humanities lecture on postmodern thought,[3] I include (in addition to a photo of a panopticon, of a scantron, and of actor Jack Nicholson as Randle Patrick McMurphy in Miloš Forman's film of One Flew Over the Cuckoo's Nest)[4] a picture of Mammy tightening the strings of Scarlett O'Hara's corset as Scarlett grabs the bedpost and yells, "Tighter!"[5] Surely such body-reshaping devices count as expressions of our willingness to conform our bodies to the power-laden ideals of the times. While we are at it, who is compelling so many people to live their lives en route to or from their body workouts?

Finally, of course, our lives on Facebook would offer supreme grist to the mill of Foucauldian analysis. Mea culpa.

The point is that Foucault helps us see what is there. It doesn't have to be all that is there (as per a reductivist account) to be worth understanding and understanding about ourselves and our time. It doesn't have to be an account that is free of a kind of base-level incoherence in order to be listened to—especially if the incoherence is noted to be endemic to the milieu that it voices and that we ourselves participate in (as I do Facebook). And especially if the incoherence itself cries out for diagonalizing resolution that only Christianity effects.

But in my humanities PowerPoint I also have a slide or two on Christianity and Pomo, including the matter of power. Christians of all people should understand in all humility the power-knowledge nexus, good and evil (discipleship, formation, justice [and injustice], mercy, also spiritual and psychological

---

3. I coordinate and team-teach in Geneva College's core course, Humanities 303.

4. Here I follow James K. A. Smith's choice of this film to epitomize Foucault's claims in chapter 4 of Who's Afraid of Postmodernism: Taking Derrida, Lyotard, and Foucault to Church (Grand Rapids: Baker, 2006).

5. Gone with the Wind, of course. 1939 film directed by Victor Fleming, from the book by Margaret Mitchell.

abuse, domestic violence, Black Lives Matter, and #MeToo), and the surpassing aptness of subversive game-changers (the cross).

So I myself have been pursuing Watkin's agenda, which he carries out admirably in this book. The agenda predates both of us by millennia. Early Christian believers read the pagan philosophers and said (something like), "Hey, this stuff is amazing!" They also said, "Hey, the Christian religion actually helps the pagan philosophers better their philosophy." Christianity makes for a better Platonism, a better Aristotelianism. This isn't meant as a contest, but as a dignity-conferring affirmation and consideration, and a generously hospitable collaboration. Truth is simple, but it's also more complex and profound and inexhaustive and objective than modernity has misled us to imagine.

As the Pevensies came to understand the existence of a deeper Magic, Scripture opens our eyes to a deeper power. "Something greater than Solomon is here" (Luke 11:31). It's a matter not of more power, but of power of a qualitatively different kind. It does not arm; it disarms—double meaning intended. Whatever the power of power in modernism, the power of Christ breaks in and breaks open, doing it transformatively, freeingly, better. One of my favorite parts of Watkin's treatise is his list of the Bible's reversals! "My soul doth magnify the Lord" (Luke 1:46 KJV)!

Victor Hugo understood this: Les Miserables famously begins with Jean Valjean's theft of the altar candlesticks. When police capture Valjean and force him before his "accuser," Bishop Myriel says to them, "You misunderstood—I gave them to him." Myriel understands that this courageous gesture of regard and love so subverts Valjean's being that his soul has now been claimed for God. Our lives may be blessed to be agents of such subversions! As Watkin clearly understands and models, one key subversion is to listen and therein accord dignity to the other. Truth must be invited hospitably. In fact, don't you see how just this little assertion gently and winsomely disarms the internalized dominance nexus that typifies modernity?

Take up and read. Follow Christopher Watkin's good example of listening, having your eyes opened, deepening your philosophical awareness and your sense of the gospel, your own need of it, and the strategically joyous gesture it is in our time. Jesus is the answer to your sins; he's also the subversively healing answer to modernism—yours along with everyone else's.

Esther Lightcap Meek
Professor of Philosophy, Geneva College
Aliquippa, Pennsylvania
September 2018

ACKNOWLEDGMENTS

I am grateful to P&R's anonymous reviewer for drawing my attention to some important alterations to this text, and to Evan Knappenberger and Nate Shannon, who provided timely and valuable advice about deficiencies in the typescript. Special thanks go to Mark Kelly, whose careful reading and incisive comments on Part 1 saved me many blushes and enhanced my understanding of key Foucauldian concepts.

My warm thanks also to the students who took part in the 2017 MOOC "Postmodernism and the Bible: Derrida and Foucault." Your questions, comments, and conversations helped me to refine my thinking, both about Foucault and about the Bible, and I am thrilled at the way you threw yourselves into the intellectual exchange. Chapeau!

For your encouragement, incisive questions, careful reading, and wise counsel, Alison, thank you. You have my unending love and admiration.

ABBREVIATIONS

ABHS   "About the Beginning of the Hermeneutics of Self:
            Two Lectures at Dartmouth"

AK   *The Archaeology of Knowledge*

BC   *The Birth of the Clinic*

DP   *Discipline and Punish*

ECS   "The Ethic of Care for the Self as a Practice of
            Freedom," in *The Final Foucault*

EW1-EST   *The Essential Works of Foucault, 1954–1984*, vol. 1,
            Ethics, Subjectivity, and Truth

EW2-AME   *The Essential Works of Foucault, 1954–1984*, vol. 2,
            Aesthetics, Method, and Epistemology

EW3-P   *The Essential Works of Foucault, 1954–1984*, vol. 3,
            Power

FL   *Foucault Live*

FR   *The Foucault Reader*

GS   "The Gay Science"

HM   *History of Madness*

HS1	*The History of Sexuality*, vol. 1, *An Introduction*
HS2	*The History of Sexuality*, vol. 2, *The Use of Pleasure*
HS3	*The History of Sexuality*, vol. 3, *The Care of the Self*
LCF-A	*Lectures at the Collège de France, 1974–1975: Abnormal*
LCF-BBP	*Lectures at the Collège de France, 1978–1979: The Birth of Biopolitics*
LCF-CT	*Lectures at the Collège de France, 1983–1984: The Courage of Truth (The Government of Self and Others II)*
LCF-PP	*Lectures at the Collège de France, 1973–1974: Psychiatric Power*
LCF-SMD	*Lectures at the Collège de France, 1975–76: Society Must Be Defended*
LCF-STP	*Lectures at the Collège de France 1977–1978: Security, Territory, Population*
LCF-WK	*Lectures at the Collège de France, 1970–1971: The Will to Know*
LCP	*Language, Counter-Memory, Practice*
OT	*The Order of Things*
P/K	*Power/Knowledge*
PPC	*Politics, Philosophy, Culture: Interviews and Other Writings, 1977–1984*
PSD	"Politics and the Study of Discourse," in *The Foucault Effect*
RM	*Remarks on Marx*
TPS	"Truth, Power, Self: An Interview with Michel Foucault," in *Technologies of the Self: A Seminar with Michel Foucault*

INTRODUCTION

By one 2016 measure,[6] Michel Foucault is the all-time most-cited author across every academic discipline from fine arts to hard science, with over a quarter more citations than his nearest rival[7] and leaving in his wake figures like Freud, Marx, and Einstein. Whatever measure is used, it is beyond doubt that his influence in the arts, humanities, and beyond is equal to or greater than that of any other twentieth-century figure. His reach is as broad as it is deep: the Library of Congress Online Catalog lists 1,299 books partially or wholly on Foucault, including titles such as *Foucault and Law, Foucault and Geography, Foucault and Classical Antiquity, Foucault and Education, Foucault and Fiction, Foucault and Religion,* and *Foucault and Aging.* With the publication of the volume you are currently reading, there will soon be one more

6. See "1360 Highly Cited Researchers (h>100) according to their Google Scholar Citations public profiles," available at http://www.webometrics.info/en/node/58. Data was collected during the third week of August 2016 of a BETA list of the public profiles of the most highly cited researchers (h-index larger than 100) according to their declared presence in the Google Scholar Citations database.

7. Pierre Bourdieu, in case you are wondering.

Foucault book on library shelves. So it behooves us to begin with the question: does the world really need yet another book on Foucault?

Well, yes it does—not because I have some startling new aspect of Foucault's thought to reveal, nor because I have discovered some long-lost manuscripts of his, but because the project of this book—to bring Foucault's thought into conversation with the Bible and Reformed theology—is both new and important. It is new because, as I explain below,[8] there have been many theological engagements with Foucault, but none of the sort that I am attempting here: to bring his thought into direct conversation with relevant biblical passages on the questions of history, power, and identity, and to compare the approach to those themes taken by Foucault and by Reformed biblical exegesis. This task is important because it reveals that Foucault and the Bible are fundamentally at variance in their assumptions, yet have a great deal in common.

One of the most striking similarities between Foucault and Reformed thought is methodological: no twentieth-century thinker does more than Foucault to unearth the conventions and commonplaces of our modern world, and the "presuppositional" tradition of Reformed apologetics likewise works hard to interrogate and expose the hidden assumptions undergirding modern thought. In the pages that follow, we will see affinities between Foucault and a Reformed understanding of the Bible in their respective views of history, in their critique of power, and in their construction of identity. We will also see, without cancelling out or minimizing these affinities, that Foucault and a Reformed understanding of the Bible have contrasting assumptions that subtend their commonalities. In the final analysis, I shall argue that Foucault and the Bible share a set

8. See "Interlude: Foucault and the Theologians."

of common concerns and problems to which they offer analogous but distinct responses, and that the Bible's responses tend on the whole to be more complex and multidimensional than Foucault's.

In attempting to strike up a conversation between Foucault and the Bible, it is important to respect, in each case, the kind of texts we are dealing with. So how should we characterize Foucault's writing? Well, here are three words to get us going: "Foucault writes stories." This, in part, accounts for him often being classed as a historian. His training, however, was in philosophy and psychiatry. That, in part, explains why many traditional historians reject his historical method. He writes stories, rather than, for example, elaborating philosophical theories in a systematic way or writing about a particular historical moment in isolation from its historical context. Foucault defends his stories as history, but he does not write them simply because they are history, nor does he simply repudiate the accusation that they are fictions:

> It seems to me that the possibility exists for fiction to function in truth, for a fictional discourse to induce effects of truth, and for bringing it about that a true discourse engenders or "manufactures" something that does not as yet exist, that is, "fictions" it. (*P/K*, 193)

He is right, is he not? Are not Homer's *Iliad* and *Odyssey* just as influential in shaping the West as Aristotle's *Nicomachean Ethics* or Plato's *Republic*, if not more so? Cannot myths, if believed, shape an individual and even a civilization, regardless of whether they are "true" in the sense of accurately representing a state of affairs in the world? The real world is built of such fictions, only some of which are "true" in the way we usually understand that term. So perhaps we can characterize

Foucault's thought, in a preliminary way, as an exploration of stories and world-making.

If this is how Foucault writes, then we need to follow his stories if we are to understand his thought. For this reason, it does not cut with the grain of Foucault's way of writing to structure this book around certain prominent Foucauldian sayings or "quotable quotes," as was my démarche in the Derrida volume in this Great Thinkers series. For the same reasons, it will not do either to bring Foucault's stories into conversation with isolated biblical verses or doctrines. That would be like comparing apples and the social history of the orange. We need to bring stories into conversation with stories, and bring the narratives that Foucault tells of our modern world into conversation with the narratives that the Bible tells about God, humanity, and history. Therefore, of all the different structures and approaches that a book such as this could take, I choose to focus on the biblical story of the incarnation, cross, resurrection, and ascension of Jesus Christ. This, of course, leaves much unsaid, but it is my hope that it will ensure that what is said can afford reasonable comparisons with the genre, as well as the content, of Foucault's thought.

The present book is divided into two parts, each with three chapters. Part 1 offers a synoptic summary of Foucault's thought, roughly divided into the commonly accepted periods of his work: archaeological, genealogical, and ethical. Within each period, I focus in turn on a dominant theme: history, power, and identity. In the three chapters of Part 2, then, I unfold a biblical account of the same themes, striking up a conversation with Foucault as I go. I hope that the diagrams I use throughout the book make this conversation easier to follow, both for those with little previous knowledge of Foucault and for those with no intimate acquaintance with the Bible. In the same way that this book seeks to lay a table at which both Foucault and the Bible can dine without denying either their differences or their affinities, I hope that both nonreligious Foucault scholars and Christians who are skeptical of Foucault will find in these pages a faithful and honest reflection of their own position and an open invitation to dialogue with an outlook that may initially appear to them as peculiar, objectionable, or hostile.

PART 1

FOUCAULT'S THOUGHT

1

HISTORY AND TRUTH

I am going to tell you a story, after which I will invite you to reflect on what you make of it. It is a true story, and it takes place in Paris in 1797, fewer than ten years after the storming of the Bastille and the social upheaval that followed. Its hero is a physician and psychiatrist called Philippe Pinel, "physician of the infirmaries" at the Bicêtre Hospital in Paris, an institution whose diverse inmates include criminals, those with physical diseases, pensioners, and the mentally ill. The story begins when Pinel notices that members of the latter group are forced to sleep upright, restrained with iron cuffs and collars, on chains a little too short to permit them to lie down. During their waking hours they are treated as animals and periodically put on show to satisfy the curiosity of Parisian visitors.

The climax of the story (I am telling you the short version) is straightforward enough and told often enough in histories of medicine and psychiatry: in a moment of epochal humanitarian progress, Pinel frees the mad of the Bicêtre from their barbarous chains.[1] It is remembered as a revolutionary gesture,

1. This act may have been accomplished by his predecessor as governor of the

immortalized by Charles Louis Müller in a painting of 1849 that hangs today in the entrance hall of the Académie Nationale de Médecine in Paris.[2] In Pinel's own words:

> To detain maniacs in constant seclusion, and to load them with chains; to leave them defenseless, . . . to rule them with a rod of iron, as if to shorten the term of an existence considered miserable, is a system of superintendence more distinguished for its convenience than for its humanity or its success. Experience proves that acute mania, especially when periodical, may be frequently cured by measures of mildness and moderate coercion, conjoined to a proper attention to the state of the mind.[3]

So then, what do you think of Pinel's reforms? Humanitarian? Undoubtedly. Ground-breaking? Certainly. Progress? Categorically. Pinel is almost universally hailed as a moral example, a liberator, and a humanitarian. The *Oxford Illustrated Companion to Medicine* trumpets him as one who "defied both the French public and the Revolutionary Government by unlocking the chains of his patients and prohibiting other barbaric methods" and who "introduced a raft of innovations, all designed to bring a semblance of gentleness and friendliness into their hitherto sordid lives."[4]

Bicêtre, Jean-Baptiste Pussin, as most now think. See K. W. M. Fulford et al., eds., *The Oxford Handbook of Philosophy and Psychiatry* (Oxford: Oxford University Press, 2013), 207–9.

2. Charles Louis Müller, *Philippe Pinel fait enlever les fers aux aliénés de Bicêtre en 1792* [Philippe Pinel has the mad freed from their chains at Bicêtre in 1792], 1852, oil on canvas, Académie Nationale de Médecine, Paris.

3. Quoted in Jan Ehrenwald, ed., *The History of Psychotherapy: From Healing Magic to Encounter* (London: Jason Aronson, 1991), 217.

4. Stephen Lock et al., eds., *The Oxford Illustrated Companion to Medicine* (Oxford: Oxford University Press, 2001), 75.

I am now going to ask you some very silly questions, but I beg you to indulge me and take it seriously: why do you think Pinel's reforms represent "progress"? Why do you think the former regime was "barbarous," and why do you think that removing chains from the mad at the Hôpital Bicêtre should be considered a "liberation"? Once your indignation has subsided that these questions can even be raised, think how you would offer a reasoned answer. What do you need to believe about the nature of madness, about human beings, about historical progress, and about the purposes of restraint for your reaction to be as self-evident to you as it is? And, if I may stretch your patience a little further, if you had other assumptions, might you not take a very different view, with equally strident certainty? Might there be a bigger story to tell than one of straightforward progress from barbarity to humanity?

Enter Foucault—not to argue that the former regime of chains and bestial treatment was better than Pinel's reforms, but precisely to tell this bigger story, a story that explains, not merely Pinel's heroism, but why it is that we should think him a hero today at all, why the mad were ever incarcerated to begin with, and what we are taking for granted when we talk about ideas like "progress." Foucault's aim in retelling Pinel's story— which he does in the course of *History of Madness*—is not to prove that progress or humanitarianism is meaningless, but to encourage an awareness of the nature and origin of the assumptions that stand behind the reasons we offer when forced to justify them, and to show that it could have been otherwise. Before we are in a position to appreciate what Foucault is doing with Pinel in particular, however, we need a sense of how he approaches history in general, and it is to that task that we now turn.

History: Hegel, Marx, Nietzsche

If we had to sum up Foucault's approach to history in the shortest possible formula, we could do worse than to say that he sides with Nietzsche, Bachelard, and Canguilhem against Hegel and Marx. In the rest of this chapter, I will try to explain the meaning of that condensed statement. The early nineteenth-century German philosopher Georg Friedrich Wilhelm Hegel (1770–1831) elaborated a philosophy of history that has transformed the way we think as much as any other philosophical system since Plato's. For our purposes here, the key terms in Hegel's understanding of history are "consciousness," "progress," and "totality." Hegel sees history as the grand story of "mind" or "spirit" (*Geist* in German), gradually coming to a consciousness of its own freedom. By *Geist* he means something like independent human subjectivities united in relation to each other in a particular society. One implication of Hegel's account, therefore, is that if we leave human consciousness out of the equation, we can never come to an adequate understanding of history. Consciousness is central to Hegel's view of history.

In order to trace how *Geist* progressively comes to a realization of its own nature, Hegel tells a story that runs from the very first ancient civilizations to his own day. The story is one of inexorable progress, but that progress is not linear. It follows a three-stage process that has come to be called "dialectic":

1. The stage of "understanding." Two concepts are accepted as fixed and mutually exclusive. For example, "being" and "nonbeing": something cannot both be and not be at the same time.
2. The stage of "dialectical reason." The concepts are seen to harbor contradictions. For example, if "being" and

"nonbeing" are absolute, how can anything ever come into being or cease to be?

3. The stage of "speculation" or "sublation."[5] The two categories from the stage of understanding are "sublated" or "passed over," and a new, higher category embraces them and resolves the apparent contradiction uncovered at stage 2. For example, "becoming" embraces both "being" and "nonbeing," and accounts for the seeming contradiction between those two lower categories.

So whereas linear progress advances in a straight line from A to B, dialectical progress advances from A and B to C. The three stages are sometimes labelled "thesis," "antithesis," and "synthesis," but Hegel uses these terms only in his critique of Kant, never in relation to his own thinking. For our purposes in this book, the main point we need to take away from Hegel's dialectical understanding of history is that historical progress, whatever its precise nature, is inexorable and inevitable: the dialectical movement rolls onward just as surely as objects fall downward, and the whole of world history is moving toward a particular goal, namely the self-realization of *Geist*.

So far, we have seen that Hegel's account of history privileges consciousness and includes a notion of inexorable progress over time. A final aspect of his thinking that we need to be familiar with before we move on to Foucault is that no development is left outside the dialectical movement: everything that happens in history can be understood in terms of the grand story of *Geist*'s self-realization, with no remainder. Hegel's philosophy seeks to account for the totality of human history, not for this or that isolated civilization or century.

5. Sublation, for Hegel (German: *Aufhebung*), draws together a complex set of meanings and is notoriously hard to define. To cut to the chase, we can think of it as resolution of contradiction in a higher unity.

Marx, for his part, adopts the basic scaffolding of Hegel's philosophy of history—the idea that history is inevitably progressing toward a particular goal—but he gets rid of the idea of *Geist* in favor of a "dialectical materialism" that focuses not on human consciousness but on economic conditions. History can still be understood as progress toward an inevitable goal, but that goal is now understood as the proletarian revolution that, in time, will usher in the classless society.

Foucault's understanding of history, to begin with, is a rejection of Hegel and Marx in the three key areas of consciousness, progress, and totality:

- For Foucault, human consciousness is not at the center of history. Traditional historiography gravitates to history's big names like Galileo, Descartes, or Martin Luther King, seeing these august figures as the primary agents of historical development. Foucault dismisses this sort of history as "doxology," an unwarranted genuflection at the altar of the "great men" of the past. He takes us to a level more fundamental than the sayings and actions of great men, a level he calls a "positive unconscious of knowledge" (*OT*, xi), which we shall explore at length below. In fact, great women and men play a rather peripheral role for Foucault, and the main historical actors are concepts, not people. The philosophical landscape of Foucault's day was divided between the philosophers of consciousness (primarily Sartre and the existentialists), and the philosophers of the concept (Gaston Bachelard and Georges Canguilhem). Foucault sides squarely with the philosophers of the concept.
- Foucault rejects the idea that history should be understood in terms of inexorable, cumulative, and irreversible progress from one age to the next, and he rejects the idea

that history is moving ever closer to a particular, prede-
termined goal. Dismissive of Hegel's and Marx's claims
to have provided a convincing account of historical
progress, he quipped that "Marxism exists in nineteenth-
century thought as a fish exists in water; that is, it ceases to
breathe anywhere else" (*OT*, 285). In his systematic rejection of Hegel, Foucault substantially aligns himself with
the approach to history taken by the nineteenth-century
German philosopher Friedrich Nietzsche—or at least
with Foucault's own reading of Nietzsche.[6] Against the
traditional way in which history seeks to explain continuities over time and seeks to account for how one thing led
to another, Foucault's Nietzsche rejects the "antiquarian
history" that consists in establishing continuities from one
event to the next, opposing it to his own "genealogy" or
"effective history," the purpose of which "is not to discover
the roots of our identity, but to commit itself to its dissi-
pation" as it labors to "make visible all of those discontinuities that cross us" (*LCP*, 162). Nietzsche's genealogical
method seeks to sniff out history's false universals (such as
"rationality")—notions that are presented as eternal and
natural, but which in fact are confined within particular
cultures and often serve the interests of a given culture's
dominant groups (*LCP*, 158). Bachelard and Canguilhem,
working on the history of science, similarly saw the ideas
of Einstein not as a gradual progression from what had
come before, but as an abrupt and dramatic rupture,[7] and

6. Foucault's reading of Nietzsche is disputed by much Nietzsche scholarship.
See, for example, Keith Ansell-Pearson, "Introduction: On Nietzsche's Critique of
Morality," in *"On the Genealogy of Morality" and Other Writings*, by Friedrich Nietzsche,
ed. Keith Ansell-Pearson (Cambridge: Cambridge University Press, 2007), xx.

7. See, for example, Gaston Bachelard, *The New Scientific Spirit*, trans. Arthur
Goldhammer (Boston: Beacon Press, 1984), 54.

from such ruptures developed an understanding of history as a succession of epistemological breaks. History had always included discussion of ruptures and discontinuities, but for Nietzsche, Bachelard, and Canguilhem, they were placed for the first time at its center.

- Foucault's histories do not assume that the stories they tell are the only possible ones or the ones that account for all historical details. As we shall see below, Foucault's main aim is not to be comprehensive and total, but to tell stories that highlight certain features of society and, especially in his later writing, achieve certain political ends. Like Nietzsche, Bachelard, and Canguilhem, Foucault privileges difference over similarity, arguing that "the freeing of difference requires thought without contradiction, without dialectics, without negation; thought that accepts divergence" (*LCP*, 185). He does not think that any account of history can or should pretend to totality: no story can be the story of everything, and we must content ourselves to tell local and limited histories confined to particular aspects of particular historical ages. Furthermore, we must tell those stories, not in terms of ideas that remain unchanged from one age to the next (which he calls "anthropological universals," *EW2-AME*, 461), but in terms of ruptures and interruptions.

The focus of Foucault's history, then, is not on how we move from one historical period to another, but on what it is about historical periods that makes them truly different in the first place. Foucault approaches history as a series of discrete snapshots, not as a movie with a scrupulous continuity editor. So the question we now need to ask of Foucault's thought is: what does a history that rejects consciousness, progress, and totality look like?

Archaeology and Epistemes

Two broad theoretical terms will help us to answer this question, and they will act as signposts along our route through the first period of Foucault's work: "archaeology" and "episteme."

Archaeology

Foucault's historical method—implicit in *History of Madness* (1961) and explicitly called "archaeology" in *The Birth of the Clinic* (1963), *The Order of Things* (1966), and *The Archaeology of Knowledge* (1969)—does not begin at thirty thousand feet with grand stories like the rise and fall of nations, or with universal concepts like empire, *Geist*, or destiny. It begins on the ground, scrutinizing particular forms of behavior:

> Instead of deducing concrete phenomena from universals, or instead of starting with universals as an obligatory grid of intelligibility for certain concrete practices, I would like to start with these concrete practices and, as it were, pass these universals through the grid of these practices. (*LCF-BBP*, 3)

Consistent with Foucault's rejection of Hegelian history, archaeology does not concern itself with the intentions and actions of human beings, but with the rules that govern what can and cannot be said and accepted at a particular moment in history—rules that operate below the level of consciousness. Whereas traditional history might concern itself with *what was said* at particular historical moments (e.g., Julius Caesar declares, "I came, I saw, I conquered," or Martin Luther King proclaims from the steps of the Lincoln Memorial, "I have a dream"), Foucault focuses rather on *what could have been said* at a particular time: what it was possible, thinkable, or permitted to say.

The rules governing such possibilities are never explicit in the historical moment in which they operate, but they are assumed unquestioningly (and most often unconsciously) by those who live in it. This is why Foucault can say that archaeology studies "the unthought" of an epoch (see *OT*, 351–58). Furthermore, these "rules" or "laws" are not written down and policed, like a penal code. They are not rules like "Do not murder," but more like "When I speak without coercion, the thoughts I express are my own." These rules are so fundamental to the way that we live, experience the world and interact with others, that we would have a very hard time conceiving that things could possibly be otherwise. It is not correct to say that we "obey" these rules in any conscious sense, nor that we recognize them as limiting us. On the contrary, we need to presuppose them in order to make sense of anything, to do anything meaningful, or to produce what we call "truth."

This focus on the assumptions necessary for meaningful speech and action situates Foucault in proximity to Immanuel Kant, but at the same time significantly distant from him. It is a proximity and distance worth noting with particular care, because the ways in which Foucault departs from Kant are very important for coming to terms with his archaeological method. In his *Critique of Pure Reason*, Kant claims to set down the "conditions of possibility" for our thinking: the categories in terms of which anything that we can think must be thought. There are twelve such categories for Kant: unity, plurality, totality, reality, negation, limitation, inherence and subsistence, causality and dependence, community, possibility, existence, and necessity. Kant calls these the "a priori" conditions of thought, meaning that they are in place before we think or observe anything at all, and without them we could not make sense of anything. For Kant, these a priori conditions are unchanging: they are the same for us as they were for our earliest ancestors, and they will remain until the final generation of our descendants.

While Foucault agrees with Kant that there are conditions

shaping what can be thought, he differs crucially from Kant when he maintains that these conditions can change over time. What it was possible meaningfully to think in thirteenth-century Paris is not the same as what it is possible meaningfully to think in twenty-first century Paris. Hence, Foucault speaks of the "historical a priori" (*AK*, 126–31). As Jeffrey Nealon points out in his treatment of this term, "historical a priori" captures something of the tension and complexity of Foucault's thought: archaeology is objective insofar as it seeks to discern the a priori conditions of thought in a particular period, but it is relative insofar as its a priori is historical.[8] We shall return to this delicate juxtaposition of the relative and the objective more than once in this book.

Epistemes

Foucault introduces the term "episteme" in *The Order of Things* to describe the most important rules governing the formation of ideas in a given historical context. He describes the term in the following way:

> What I am attempting to bring to light is the epistemological field, the *episteme* in which knowledge, envisaged apart from all criteria having reference to its rational value or to its objective forms, grounds its positivity and thereby manifests a history which is not that of its growing perfection, but rather that of its conditions of possibility. . . . Such an enterprise is not so much a history, in the traditional meaning of that word, as an "archaeology." (*OT*, xxiii–xxiv)

An episteme, then, is an "epistemological field," a space in which knowledge can be produced according to particular rules.

8. Jeffrey T. Nealon, "Historical a Priori," in *The Cambridge Foucault Lexicon*, ed. Leonard Lawlor and John Nale (Cambridge: Cambridge University Press, 2014), 200–206.

Although there is some disagreement in the secondary literature about whether epistemes can coexist, in *The Order of Things*
Foucault indicates that each historical epoch has one (and only
one) episteme (*OT*, 168), stretching across all academic disciplines as well as conditioning everyday thought.

All of this makes an episteme sound very much like a worldview, but it is a comparison that Foucault resists. As a good anti-
Hegelian, he rejects the unifying and totalizing notion of worldview,
insisting in the lecture "Politics and the Study of Discourse" that
"'I do not seek to detect . . . the unitary spirit of an epoch" and that
"the episteme is not a sort of grand underlying theory, it is a space
of dispersion, it is an open and doubtless indefinitely describable
field of relationships" (*PSD*, 55) between different discourses.
Epistemes serve not to integrate but to disperse, and "archaeological comparison does not have a unifying, but a diversifying, effect"
(*AK*, 160). To use a rather crude and approximate electronic metaphor to sit alongside Foucault's own images of an "intellectual
unconscious" and "historical a priori," we might say that, whereas
traditional history concerns itself with the software that happens to
be running in a particular epoch, Foucault investigates the capabil-
ities and limits of the underlying programming language. Whereas
the episteme (programming language) sets the conditions of what
can and cannot be thought and said, actual statements (software)
are a record of what has in fact been said.

In a moment, we shall take a look at *History of Madness* in
more detail, but first of all it will be useful to familiarize ourselves
with Foucault's archaeological method by setting out his broad
understanding of the three historical epistemes that he considers
in *The Order of Things*: Renaissance, Classical, and modern.

The Renaissance Episteme

The episteme of the Renaissance (fifteenth-century Florence
to seventeenth-century Europe) is characterized by similitude,

affinities, and correspondences. Of primary importance to the Renaissance way of understanding the world is that different parts of the universe resemble and correspond to each other in fundamental ways. Foucault uses the rather charming example of aconite, a dark-blue flowering plant, the seeds of which "are tiny dark globes set in white skin-like coverings whose appearance is much like that of eyelids covering an eye" (*OT*, 30–31). For the Renaissance mind, this resemblance between aconite and the eye is no coincidence: the correspondence indicates an affinity, which means that the plant can be used to cure ocular diseases. In a similar way, it is no surprise for the Renaissance mind, nor mere poetic conceit, that the night of Banquo's murder in *Macbeth* should be accompanied by stormy weather. Duncan's attendant Lennox describes the night of the murder in the following terms:

> LENNOX: Where we lay,
> Our chimneys were blown down and, as they say,
> Lamentings heard i' th' air, strange screams of death,
> And prophesying with accents terrible
> Of dire combustion and confused events
> New hatched to th'woeful time.[9]

It is quite understandable for Lennox and the other characters that there should be a causal connection between a disturbance in the social order (Banquo's murder) and the natural order (the violent wind), just as there is an affinity between aconite and the eye.

The Classical Episteme

Around the middle of the seventeenth century, the Renaissance episteme comes to an end. Foucault does not tell

---

9. William Shakespeare, *Macbeth*, 2.3.43–51.

us why, for he is writing a Nietzschean history of ruptures, not a Hegelian history of continuity and progress. The Classical episteme no longer understands the world in terms of similitude and affinity, but in terms of representation, taxonomy, and mathematical calculation. The world is no longer to be interpreted (as, for example, in the case of aconite and the eye), but measured and classified. Language, which for the Renaissance episteme was an autonomous reality that participated in the same similitudes and correspondences as everything else, now becomes external to things. The relation between language and the world is no longer a natural one; rather, language is now assumed to explain things from a distance, imitating them more or less accurately. For this new, Classical episteme, to conceive of something is to represent it in the mind, a paradigm epitomized in Descartes' *cogito ergo sum*: "I am thinking, therefore I exist."

The transition from the Renaissance to the Classical episteme is captured for Foucault in Miguel de Cervantes's 1615 novel *Don Quixote*. The eponymous knight errant sets out on a quest, expecting to discover resemblances and correspondences between the heroic tales of chivalry he has read and the countryside in which he travels, but instead he finds himself in a world of measurement and representation, stripped of the romance and interconnectedness that the Renaissance episteme affords.

The Modern Episteme

Foucault discerns a further epistemic shift around the beginning of the nineteenth century, this time from the Classical to the modern. The rupture is characterized by a growing understanding of the limits of Classical representation. The Classical age thought that language and measurement could adequately represent the world (in terms of Descartes' *cogito*, it thought that the "I am thinking" could adequately represent the "I" that exists), but the modern age begins to see that reality cannot adequately be thus represented. In the same way that Foucault locates Cervantes at the hinge of the Renaissance and the Classical, he situates artist Diego Velázquez and author the Marquis de Sade on the cusp of the modern.

Foucault devotes the first section of *The Order of Things* to Velázquez's painting *Las Meninas*, insisting that, when viewing this canvas, the gallery visitor cannot place herself in any position that makes comprehensive sense of its lines of perspective and reflections, with the result that "no gaze is stable" (*OT*, 5). This would not have been a problem for the Classical age, Foucault argues, as it did not consider the way in which reflecting upon the position of the viewing subject complicates what is being

Fig. 1.1. Diego Velázquez, *Las Meninas* [*The Ladies-in-Waiting*], 1656, oil on canvas, 318 cm × 276 cm, Museo del Prado, Madrid.

viewed; it is only in the modern episteme that the one for whom the world is represented is called into question. Indeed, the subject (and "man" more broadly) comes to the fore in the modern episteme such that Foucault can famously say, in the final section of *The Order of Things*, that "man is an invention of recent date. And one perhaps nearing its end" (*OT*, 422).

The appearance of "man" in the modern age can also be seen, for Foucault, in Kant's categories of the understanding, sketched above. For Kant, it is the human subject who shapes and gives content to reality, rather than merely representing it. As for Sade, his attempts to capture erotic excess are "no longer the ironic triumph of representation over resemblance," but rather "the obscure and repeated violence of desire battering at the limits of representation" (*OT*, 288). With Sade, we see language finding its limits, grasping at that which it cannot represent, and therefore becoming a problem in a way that was not evident in the Classical age. This parallels the way in which Velázquez shows us the limitations of the viewing subject, making the subject of representation a problem in a way in which it previously was not.

Language in the modern age once more became autonomous. Rather than merely imitating reality, as it did in the Classical age, the nineteenth century sees language not as a window through which we can see reality, but as a medium that always leaves a remainder when it tries to capture the meaning of the world. The "dark, concave, inner side" (*OT*, 258) of representation takes on great importance. The Cartesian *cogito* also loses its transparency and self-evidence in the modern age: the symmetry between "I am thinking" and "I exist" is broken, and I can no longer know myself apart from the shadows and opacities of the unthought. Foucault remains silent on the question of what might succeed the modern episteme, hinting only that Nietzsche is the one who can lead us beyond it.

History of Madness (1961)[10]

It is now time to engage more closely with one of the major texts from the early period of Foucault's writing in order to acquaint ourselves with some of the characteristic moves and positions of his thought. In *History of Madness*,[11] Foucault implicitly follows what he would later call his archaeological method to analyze the history of madness in the West from the Renaissance to the modern day. Before we look at the book in detail, let us spend an important moment considering in broad terms what *History of Madness* is about and, equally importantly, what it is not about. *History of Madness* is not the history of the asylum. Nor is it about an ahistorical, universal, overarching reality that is called "madness" in one age, "unreason" in another, and "mental illness" in a third. This would be too much of a continuous, totalizing, Hegelian understanding of history for Foucault's Nietzschean sensibilities. What Foucault is seeking to write is a history of concepts, behaviors, and practices—different ways in which "madness" has been understood and dealt with in the modern West. In line with his commitment to begin, not with universal ideas, but with particular behaviors and practices, Foucault rejects the idea that madness is an ahistorical given that transcends different epochs—periods that in some later works he will call epistemes. As he later explained, looking back at *History of Madness*: "If we suppose that it [i.e., a universal, ahistorical concept of madness] does not exist, then what can history

10. Foucault's *Folie et déraison: Histoire de la folie à l'âge classique* was originally published in 1961. A version with a new preface and two appendices was brought out with the title *Histoire de la folie à l'âge classique* in 1972, from which the English translation *History of Madness* is taken.

11. The French title of the 1972 revised edition of the text is *Histoire de la folie à l'âge classique*. This poses a problem for English translators, because "folie" has a broad semantic range, translating both the "madness" of the Shakespearean fool and the "insanity" of modern medicine.

make of these different events and practices which are apparently organized around something that is supposed to be madness?" (*LCF-BBP*, 3).

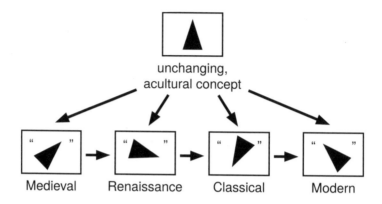

Fig. 1.2. Foucault does not conceive of the history of madness in terms of particular, historically and culturally limited ways of referring to overarching and essentially unchanging concepts outside of culture and time.

It will not simply do, however, to get rid of the overarching concept in order to leave a succession of historically limited notions:

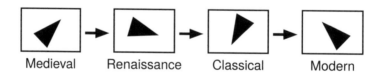

Fig. 1.3. Foucault does not conceive of the history of madness in terms of a succession of discrete and equivalent individual concepts, historically and culturally bound.

The problem with this model is that it assumes that these terms can be understood apart from the broader historical moment in which they arise. It treats them as atomistic meanings that can be isolated, captured, and individually pinned by the historical lepidopterist. This approach assumes that "madness," for example, occupies the same conceptual space for one historical period as "mental illness" does for another, which is precisely the sort of universalism that Foucault wants to contest. The whole point of the archaeological method is not to take these terms out of their original contexts, but to see how they function in relation to other concepts within their cultural-historical moment:[12]

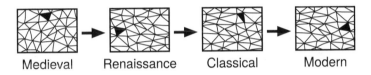

Medieval   Renaissance   Classical   Modern

Fig. 1.4. The concepts in a particular historical period can only be understood in relation to other concepts in that period, and do not necessarily have direct and exact equivalents in other periods.

With this understanding of the nature and importance of historical ways of thinking (later to be called "epistemes") in place, let us now go on to see how Foucault tells the story of madness.

Renaissance Madness

Before the Renaissance, Foucault argues, madness was not treated as a distinct category; it was not the negation or opposite of reason, but one among many possibilities of human experience, occupying a "liminal situation . . . in medieval society"

12. This is one of the reasons that Foucault has frequently been branded a structuralist. It is a label he sometimes embraced, sometimes repudiated. For an excellent discussion of Foucault's complex relation to the label "structuralism," see Patrick Singy, "Structuralism," in *The Cambridge Foucault Lexicon*, ed. Lawlor and Nale, 490–95.

(*HM*, 11). Foucault's story really starts with the Renaissance. Indeed, he begins the opening chapter of *History of Madness* with a discussion of a striking image that "made its appearance in the imaginary landscape of the Renaissance" and soon "occupied a privileged place there" (*HM*, 8): the highly symbolic "ship of fools" (*stultiferia navis*). Ships of fools, says Foucault, sailed around medieval Europe with their singular cargo, namely "the senseless in search of their reason" (*HM*, 10).

Foucault does not begin *History of Madness* by discussing the ship of fools simply to grab the reader's attention (though it certainly does that). He is signaling his anti-Hegelian archaeological method: he begins, not with overarching theories or concepts, but with particular behaviors and practices. He begins, as it were, at ground level and only afterward works up to a more general understanding of a historical period.

During the Renaissance, Foucault says, madness was thought to play a subversive role in society. It taught an instructive lesson about the future overturning of the established order (in this case, the order of reason) in God's final judgment at the end of time, and the ships of fools sailed around Europe as "a paradise regained of sorts, as men once more become strangers to necessity and want, yet without a return to a state of innocence" (*HM*, 20). The mad were seen to mock the fragility of human reason and to carry a strange wisdom, the wisdom that falls from the mouth of fools in Shakespeare's plays: Feste in *Twelfth Night*, the Fool in *King Lear*, or Hamlet himself.

Classical Madness: The Great Confinement

The term most characteristic of madness in the Classical age for Foucault is "the great confinement": the internment of the mad in hospitals and former lazar houses (institutions for the care of lepers). The Classical age no longer considered madness a source of wisdom or an eschatological subversion of reason, nor was it thought to yield any pedagogical benefit for the sane. Madness also lost the theological significance it held during the Renaissance, during which time faith in Christ crucified was held to be, in the language of 1 Corinthians 1, foolishness (Greek: *moria*), a form of spiritual madness. The sense of sanctified madness completely disappeared in the Classical age:

> When Classical Christianity spoke of the madness of the Cross, it was to expose false reasoning and bring the eternal light of the truth out into the open: the madness of God-made man was wisdom that the men of this world failed to recognize in the unreason that ruled this world. . . . "Do not despair, if the cross which has brought the universe into submission to you is the madness and scandal of proud spirits." (*HM*, 152)

Classical madness, by contrast, was purely and simply the negation and absence of reason. The mad were simply shorn of rationality—a capacity that in this period was considered the defining human characteristic—and were thus reduced to a state of animality: "The animal in man was no longer the indicator of a beyond, but had become in itself his madness, with no reference to anything other than itself, his madness in a natural state" (*HM*, 148). Whereas Renaissance society could identify with the mad as a particularly striking image of the fragility of its own reason, in the Classical age no affinity remained between the mad and the sane.

Whereas the Renaissance viewed madness as a transient stage through which one could pass, the Classical age considered it a one-way street: the mad could not be cured and were to be separated from the rest of the population, confined with other miscreants such as criminals, the licentious, and vagabonds. Furthermore, the mad were thought to be responsible for their condition and, correspondingly, madness was treated in a way appropriate for those who had voluntarily given up their humanity and who, along with the other "unreasonable" groups, refused to work and contribute to the general prosperity and order of society: they were punished and made to perform forced labor. It follows that, when the mad were put on show before curious visitors, it was not merely as a form of entertainment, but as an object lesson in the consequences of choosing the path of unreason, much in the same way that today an ex-offender might address a high school class in order to warn the children of the dangers of choosing a life of crime. The catchall category of "unreason" may strike us today as bizarre, if not cruel—grouping together, as it does, the mad, criminals, and libertines—but this is an indication of just how much our own episteme differs from that of our seventeenth-century forebears.

Modern Madness: The Age of the Asylum

At the point of transition from the Classical to the modern age, we find the reforms of Philippe Pinel and his English Quaker counterpart, Samuel Tuke. Breaking the chains of the "great confinement," Pinel and Tuke ushered in what Foucault calls "the age of the asylum," when madness ceased to be a judicial category and became a medical concern. Whereas the Classical "hospital" was a place of confinement and punishment, the modern asylum is a place of treatment and cure; whereas the hospital housed the mad together with criminals, vagabonds, and libertines, the asylum separates them from these other groups.

What Foucault wants to question in his account of madness in the modern age is not the fact that Pinel and Tuke pioneered the liberation of the mad from their chains, but the meanings attached to such a liberation. Although "[Pinel's] gesture was always seen as a 'liberation' of the mad," Foucault suggests that "in fact it was something quite different" (*HM*, 481). Pinel and Tuke did not, Foucault argues, liberate the mad from the chains in order that they might enjoy a state of freedom; they merely moved them from one condition of confinement to a new, more intrusive and more rigorous captivity. The new chains were not physical, but mental; they consisted in the process by which, in the asylum, the mad person was "forced to feel responsible for all within [his sickness] that could trouble morality and good society" (*HM*, 484), and to feel this way in the context of a regime which "substituted the stifling responsibility of anguish for the free terror of madness" (*HM*, 485). In other words, during the Classical age the restraint on the mad was exterior: shackles prevented them from circulating in society and from disturbing the other inhabitants of the hospitals. What the asylum now achieves, however, is an internalization of these controls and constraints: the mad are forced to experience their own condition as a form of mental illness, and they are made to police and control themselves in a much more invasive and intimate way than iron chains ever could. To borrow a term from Foucault's later *Discipline and Punish*, the mad are taught to "normalize" themselves (to conform themselves to an idealized model of "normal" conduct, or else be punished). This new internal form of control is illustrated in the uncanny ritual of formal tea parties held at Samuel Tuke's Retreat. The directors and the keepers at the Retreat would regularly invite some of the patients to tea parties:

> All who attend, dress in their best clothes, and vie with each other in politeness and propriety. The best fare is provided, and the visitors are treated with all the attention of strangers. The evening generally passes in the greatest harmony and enjoyment. It rarely happens that any unpleasant circumstance occurs; the patients control, in a wonderful degree, their different propensities; and the scene is at once curious, and affectingly gratifying. (*HM*, 487)

Such normalization for Foucault is nothing less than the confinement of the mad within the walls—so to speak—of their own minds:

> The madman was invited to turn himself into an object for the eyes of reasonable reason, as the perfect stranger, i.e., he whose foreignness is never perceptible. The city of reasonable men only welcomes him to the extent that he conforms to that anonymous type. (*HM*, 487)

As Foucault tellingly points out, this internal incarceration preceded physical liberation and acted as its condition; one recalcitrant patient who refused to normalize herself was "tied up in a straitjacket" and spoken to "in the strongest terms" until she broke down in "a torrent of tears, which she shed for nearly two hours" (*HM*, 502). Such were the limits of the new humanitarian approach.

In addition, unlike the wise fools of the Renaissance, the mad themselves have no voice in the age of the asylum, for the "language of psychiatry" is a "monologue of reason *about* madness" (*HM*, xxviii), and the mad are reduced to being the objects of the scientific expert's ministrations. On into the twentieth century, Freudian psychoanalysis only further embeds this tendency: the mad are forced to understand their experience in terms of a preestablished psychoanalytic discourse that privileges certain causes and explanations at the same time as forbidding others, turning the voices of unreason into a symptom.

Critiques of Foucault's History

Since the publication of *History of Madness* and Foucault's other early works, a number of important critiques of his archaeological method have arisen. I can here only summarize the most important objections and indicate how Foucault has been, or could be, defended.

The first attack on Foucault's archaeology is that he does not account for the transitions from one episteme to another. In line with Nietzsche's history of disjunctions and Bachelard's and Canguilhem's understanding of the history of science, Foucault insists that these transitions are not gradual and imperceptible metamorphoses, but "sudden take-offs" and "hastenings of evolution" (*P/K*, 112), and yet he offers no account of how such changes come about. One of the most famous and most cutting formulations of this critique is Sartre's jibe that Foucault's history "replaces cinema with a slide show, movement with a succession of immobile structures."[13] In Foucault's defense, it could be argued that the whole point of his anti-Hegelian (and anti-Sartrean) approach is to disrupt the idea of a smooth, unbroken, and inevitable movement from one era to the next, and so to answer Sartre's critique on its own terms would undermine Foucault's own view of history. It should also be pointed out that Foucault did address this problem more (though not to everyone's satisfaction) in his later, genealogical work.

Second, Foucault's writing has been interrogated on empirical grounds. Critics have insisted that things simply did not happen as he claims. This position was powerfully and influentially argued by the American historian H. C. Erik Midelfort, commenting on the abridged translation of *Histoire de la folie à l'âge Classique*, published in 1964 as *Madness and Civilization*: "What we have discovered in looking at *Madness and Civilization* is that many of its arguments fly in the face of empirical evidence, and that many of its broadest generalizations are oversimplifications."[14] The list of specific charges against Foucault is

13. Jean-Paul Sartre, "Jean-Paul Sartre répond," *L'arc* 30 (1966): 87. CW's translation.

14. Erik Midelfort, "Madness and Civilization in Early Modern Europe: A

large: Europe was in fact not crisscrossed by ships of fools, and Foucault's description of these ships as full of "the senseless in search of their reason" (*HM*, 10) is pure invention; the mad began to be confined well before the Classical age; the great confinement was about poverty, not madness; the mad were not confined during the Classical age; there was no new understanding of the relation between reason and madness at the end of the great confinement; Foucault's whole account is Francocentric, etc.

How can Foucault respond to these empirical criticisms? Part of the answer is to remember what Foucauldian archaeology is doing, namely, mapping what was thinkable in a particular period. So although there may not have been ships of fools queuing up along the waterways of Europe, the image of the ship of fools was still prominent in Renaissance art and figured in the public imagination. More broadly, the empirical distinction between fact and fiction is not Foucault's primary concern:

> I am well aware that I have never written anything but fictions. I do not mean to say, however, that truth is therefore absent. It seems to me that the possibility exists for fiction to function in truth, for a fictional discourse to induce effects of truth, and for bringing it about that a true discourse engenders or "manufactures" something that does not as yet exist, that is, "fictions" it. (*P/K*, 193)

Foucault is not in the first instance asking, "What really happened?" but, "What accounts for the way in which people thought?" Also, epistemes can be formed just as much of images and fictions as they can of empirically verifiable facts.

Reappraisal of Michel Foucault," in *After the Reformation: Essays in Honour of J. H. Hexter*, ed. Barbara C. Malament (Manchester: Manchester University Press, 1980), 259.

A third critique of Foucault as a historian is that the rejection of the idea of progress in his disjunctive account of history leaves him with a pessimistic and nihilistic view in which it becomes impossible to say that one episteme is "better" than another, evacuating any possibility of Foucault's thought being pressed into the service of political emancipation or resistance. Foucault's response to this accusation, recorded in a visit to Berkeley in the year before he died, is instructive and worth quoting at length:

> I don't think that to be suspicious means that you don't have any hope. Despair and hopelessness are one thing; suspicion is another. And if you are suspicious, it is because, of course, you have a certain hope. The problem is to know which kind of hope you have and which kind of hope it is reasonable to have in order to avoid what I would call not the "pessimistic circle" you speak of but the political circle which introduces in your hopes, and through your hopes, the things you want to avoid by these hopes.[15]

Foucault insists that his understanding of history does not issue in pessimism; rather, it makes it clear that things could be otherwise, that the present is contingent, and that no order or way of thinking is necessary, least of all our current one. Far from putting a dampener on the possibility of political activism and social transformation, archaeology provides a context in which such changes can and do take place. Just what form such a transformation might take we will explore more fully in chapter 3.

Fourth, there is what we might call the *tu quoque* (Latin: "you also") critique. If Foucault is correct, then he is just as bound by his own episteme as anyone else, which undermines any claim

15. Jeremy Carrette quotes this passage in the foreword to *Religion and Culture: Michel Foucault* (London: Routledge, 2013), xiv, where he refers to it as "an unpublished part of a discussion with several Americans at Berkeley."

on his part to give an impartial account of different epistemic epochs. Foucault readily admits that his own writing depends on "conditions and rules of which [he was] very largely unaware" (*OT*, xv), and he affirms that we cannot adequately describe our own archive (i.e., our own historical moment) because we are part of it (*AK*, 130). When this critique is used as a way to probe Foucault's analyses, it certainly has merit; when it is used as an excuse not to think seriously at all about what he is saying, it is an intellectual cop-out.

This brief survey of critiques of Foucault's historical method brings us to the end of our journey through his archaeological period. We turn now to his writing during the 1970s, commonly designated "genealogical." It is both a continuation and a revision of his archaeological approach, and it is the period when we see the theme of power relations take center stage.

2

POWER AND KNOWLEDGE

I can think of no examples more vivid or more apposite to introduce Foucault's account of power than his own famously and
startlingly contrasting figures of Damiens and Faucher at the
beginning of *Discipline and Punish*.[1] Like *History of Madness*,
Discipline and Punish begins with a striking passage that grabs
the reader's attention, and the best way to convey its force is simply to quote it. Be warned, reader: it is not for the squeamish.
Here, then, is the opening paragraph of the opening chapter of
Discipline and Punish:

> On 2 March 1757 Damiens the regicide was condemned
> "to make the *amende honorable* before the main door of the
> Church of Paris," where he was to be "taken and conveyed in
> a cart, wearing nothing but a shirt, holding a torch of burning
> wax weighing two pounds"; then, "in the said cart, to the Place
> de Grève, where, on a scaffold that will be erected there, the
> flesh will be torn from his breasts, arms, thighs and calves with

1. *Surveiller et punir: Naissance de la prison* was published by Gallimard in 1975,
translated as *Discipline and Punish: The Birth of the Prison* and published by Pantheon
Books in 1977.

red-hot pincers, his right hand, holding the knife with which he committed the said parricide, burnt with sulfur, and, on those places where the flesh will be torn away, poured molten lead, boiling oil, burning resin, wax and sulfur melted together and then his body drawn and quartered by four horses and his limbs and body consumed by fire, reduced to ashes and his ashes thrown to the winds." (*DP*, 3)

Why is Foucault telling us about the treatment of Damiens's body after his attempted assassination of King Louis XV of France in 1757? It is in order to contrast this horrific punishment (the story of which continues for a further two and a half pages) with another account, written less than a century later by the economist and politician Léon Faucher, comprising rules "For the House of young prisoners in Paris":

Art. 17. The prisoners' day will begin at six in the morning in winter and at five in summer. They will work for nine hours a day throughout the year. Two hours a day will be devoted to instruction. Work and the day will end at nine o'clock in winter and at eight in summer.

Art. 18. Rising. At the first drum-roll, the prisoners must rise and dress in silence, as the supervisor opens the cell doors. At the second drum-roll, they must be dressed and make their beds. At the third, they must line up and proceed to the chapel for morning prayer. There is a five-minute interval between each drum-roll. (*DP*, 6)

This passage from Faucher's *De la réforme des prisons* (*On Prison Reform*) (1838) continues with further articles on prayer, work, lunch, school, recreation, supper, reading, washing, and bed.

What these contrasting accounts illustrate, Foucault argues, is the difference between two different penal styles (*DP*, 7), styles that in the course of *Discipline and Punish* will be labelled as "sovereign power" and "disciplinary power," respectively. The question Foucault poses and seeks to answer is this: what accounts for this startling transformation, in a mere eighty years, from an age of pincers and sulfur to one of rising at five in the morning and making one's bed?

Is the change in practices of punishment due, perchance, to a growth of humanitarian consciousness and an abandonment of antiquated, barbarous mores? From what we already know of Foucault from *History of Madness*, we may well have an inkling that his answer will be in the negative. Doubtless this story of increased humanitarianism over time appeals to us today because it flatters our sense of ourselves as enlightened, benevolent individuals who have outgrown the barbarities both of the past and of other (non-Western) societies in our own day. Foucault, however, has a different story to tell, one that is decidedly less flattering and that adds a great deal of complexity to the simplistic tale of progress from a barbarous past to a humanitarian present.

From Archaeology to Genealogy

In the 1970s, the "archaeology" of Foucault's earlier thought was superseded by the "genealogy" of texts like *Discipline and Punish* and *The Will to Knowledge*. In addition to bringing the analysis of power relations to the fore,[2] Foucault's move from archaeology to genealogy signaled the following important methodological shifts:

2. In a 1975 interview, Foucault claims that power has been his focus all along (*EW3-P*, 283–85). He repeats this claim later in relation to subjectivity (*EW1-EST*, 289), saying that his work has always been about his current concerns at a given moment. Foucault is not entirely incorrect in his self-assessments, but they are to be understood as strategic interventions as much as informative clarifications.

- Whereas archaeology focused predominantly on language, statements, and discourse, genealogy takes into account behaviors and practices that do not have an explicitly discursive dimension.
- Partly as a result of foregrounding power relations, Foucault's genealogies are more overtly political than his earlier archaeologies, directly discussing resistance and other political themes. This is also the period of his involvement in the politics of Iran and his work with the Groupe d'information sur les prisons (Prisons Information Group) that sought to give a public platform to the first-hand testimony of inmates in French jails.
- The emphasis of genealogy for Foucault (consonant with the dictionary sense of the term) is to tell us who we are today. Foucault's genealogies seek—more prominently than do his archaeologies—to explain the history of the modern subject in order that we can better understand ourselves, with all our possibilities and limits.

What Is Power?

Power is the term perhaps most frequently associated with Foucault's thought, and it is also one of the most misunderstood. Presently we shall see that power takes many different forms over time, but for now let us try—at the risk of being reductive—to summarize what can be said of power in general. So then, what does Foucault mean by "power" and, just as importantly, what does he not mean? I offer nine theses by way of summary.

1. Power Does Not Stand Alone, but Qualifies Relations.

The first thing to notice—and it is an important starting point—is that Foucault does not understand the term "power" as a stand-alone concept. When he uses the word in isolation, he does so as shorthand for his preferred "relations of power" (*EW1-EST*, 291). In other words, power is not a commodity or object that can be separated from the relations it qualifies.

2. Power Is Not Just a Relation between Oppressor and Oppressed.

If power is to be understood not as a thing in itself but as a relation, then it would be a mistake to think that such relations are always relations of oppression. Power relations operate, Foucault insists, in chains and in a "net-like organization" (*P/K*, 98)—or what he elsewhere calls a "micro-physics of power" (*DP*, 26–29, 139), not in binary relations of masters and slaves. This rejection of the simple schema of oppressor and oppressed is also at the heart of his criticism of Marx's account of class struggle, which is a binary equation in which the powerful bourgeoisie oppresses the powerless proletariat. For Foucault, such a reductive account collapses the many different power relations operating in society into one monolithic example, whereas in fact "there is no single locus of great Refusal, no soul of revolt, source of all rebellions, or pure law of the revolutionary. Instead there is a plurality of resistances, each of them a special case" (*HS1*, 95–96).

3. Power Is Not Possessed or Held.

Individuals are not primarily sources of power, but vehicles for it or "places" where it is enacted. It is "not something that is acquired, seized, or shared, something that one holds on to or allows to slip away" (*HS1*, 94), but rather "a machine in which everyone is caught, those who exercise power just as much as those over whom it is exercised" (*P/K*, 156). In *Discipline and Punish*, Foucault refers to the "capillary functioning of power" (*DP*, 198) to evoke "a network of relations, constantly in tension, in activity, rather than a privilege that one might possess" (*DP*, 26).

4. Power Is Everywhere, but Is Not Everything.

It is a common misunderstanding that, for Foucault, every-thing is power or can be reduced to power. What he in fact says is somewhat different: "power is everywhere; not because it embraces everything, but because it comes from everywhere" (*HS1*, 93). Relations of kinship, for example, cannot be exhaus-tively reduced to power, but they have power running through them. No relation is free or exempt from power, but it would also be wrong to say that relations consist of nothing but power.

5. Power Relations Are Not Obvious.

Like Foucault's search for the "unthought" of a historical epoch in his archaeological work, his analysis of power seeks to dig beneath appearances and starts from the position that "the relations of power are perhaps among the best hidden things in the social body" (*PPC*, 118).

6. Power Is Creative, Not Repressive.

It may be Marx's idea (and indeed the dominant view in the history of political thought) that power is always repressive, but it is not Foucault's. For him, power is known primarily not through what it suppresses or constrains, but through what it creates. Primary among these creations is the human subject.

7. The Subject Is Constituted as a Reciprocal Interplay of Power and Resistance.

This seventh point helps us to avoid two mistakes in under-standing what Foucault says about power, so it is worth slowing down and explaining it more thoroughly. In trying to understand the way in which power relates to what Foucault calls "subjecti-vation"—that is, the process by which a human being becomes a self-conscious subject—it is easy to jump to one of two extremes. The first extreme is to imagine the subject as something akin to a city under siege from a foreign empire. That empire is "power," and the subject seeks valiantly to remain uncontaminated by power's effects and to resist its assaults.

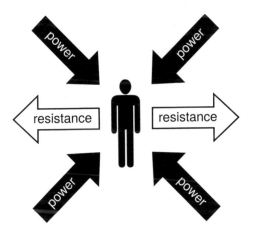

Fig. 2.1. The subject does not resist power from a position outside or before power.

But it is a grave mistake, Foucault insists, to understand the subject in this way, thinking of it "as a sort of elementary nucleus, a primitive atom or some multiple, inert matter to which power is applied, or which is struck by a power that subordinates or destroys individuals" (*LCF-SMD*, 29). It follows that "we should not, therefore, be asking subjects how, why, and by what right they can agree to being subjected, but showing how actual relations of subjection manufacture subjects" (*LCF-SMD*, 45, translation altered). In other words, the subject is not power's opposite, but its effect (*LCF-SMD*, 30).

The second error, however, is to take this statement—"the subject is not power's opposite, but its effect"—to mean that the subject itself is nothing but the passive effect of power, an object with no agency of its own that is simply produced by relations over which it has no control.

Fig. 2.2. Nor is the subject utterly passive as it is constituted by power.

The truth for Foucault lies at neither of these active and passive extremes that by turns give the subject too much and too little agency. In fact, he insists that the subject is always constituted by the interplay of power and resistance to power. As Foucault quite rightly notes, there could be no power without resistance, because power is action upon the action of others: I have not acted upon your action unless I change what you were going to do, and there can be no power exerted to make someone do what they would have done anyway. Similarly, there can be no action upon your action unless you had an action of your own to be acted upon in the first place! Conversely, there can be no resistance without power, for what, in that case, would resistance be resisting? In other words, "resistance really always relies upon the situation against which it struggles" (*EW1*, 168), and the subject is always constituted as an interplay of power and resistance.

Power and resistance require each other and grow together, rather than resistance arising after power has exerted itself: "Where there is power, there is resistance" (*HS1*, 95). Power and resistance conspire in a number of ways to give rise to the subject. First, "the individual is a relay: power passes through the individuals it has constituted" (*LCF-SMD*, 29–30), represented

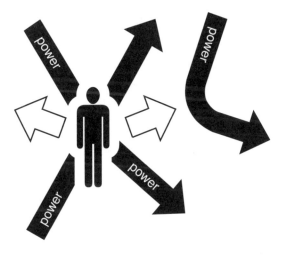

Fig. 2.3. The subject is constituted as a reciprocal interplay of power and resistance.

in Figure 2.3 by the arrows passing through the subject. This power passing through the subject, however, does not make it merely a passive object, for "power relations are obliged to change with the resistance" (*EW1*, 161). When passing through the individuals it has constituted, some power meets relatively little resistance, some meets with stronger resistance and is diverted, and some is even repelled. It is in this multilayered and necessary interplay of power and resistance—necessary because neither could exist without the other—that the subject emerges.

This account of power and resistance in the constitution of the subject has not gone unchallenged. Oliver Feltham and Justin Clemens, for example, point out that Foucault claims that "networks of disciplinary power [...] actually produce what we call subjects" and that power "produces resistance."[3] If power

3. Oliver Feltham and Justin Clemens, "An Introduction to Alain Badiou's Philosophy," in *Infinite Thought: Truth and the Return of Philosophy*, ed. and trans. Oliver Feltham and Justin Clemens (London: Continuum, 2006), 1–28, 5. Clemens

produces resistance, then how can resistance meaningfully resist power? Resistance would have to have some independence from power in order meaningfully to resist it, if its agency is to be distinguished from the power it is resisting. Feltham, Clemens and Harris conclude that this problem of the independence of resistance from power is never resolved in Foucault's work, and I find it hard to see how any different conclusion can be reached.

8. Power Does Not Distort Knowledge from the Outside: It Is Implicated in Its Creation from the Inside.

Just as power, for Foucault, does not stand over against the subject, so also it does not stand over against knowledge. For Marx (once more echoing themes to be found in most political theory before Foucault), power supervenes on knowledge from the outside in what he calls "ideology," distorting knowledge in the process. For Foucault, however, knowledge is always already "power-knowledge," an inseparable amalgam. Knowledge does not precede power and survey it from a neutral, objective position; rather, it is always already implicated in power (though the two are not the same thing, contrary to what some interpretations of Foucauldian power-knowledge assume). Foucault's notion of power-knowledge is not suggesting, let it be clearly heard, that all "truth claims" are reducible to "power plays." As Todd May helpfully puts it, "That would not be power-knowledge: it would just be power," pure and simple.[4] Foucault is claiming that there is no knowledge untouched by or unrelated to power, not that knowledge is nothing but power.

---

and Feltham's argument is quoted and summarized in Mitchell M. Harris, "Sites of Resistance: Christ and Materiality after the New Historicism," in Cassandra Falke, ed., *Intersections in Christianity and Critical Theory* (Basingstoke: Palgrave Macmillan, 2010), 56–69, 61.

4. Todd May, *The Philosophy of Foucault* (London: Routledge, 2014), 76.

9. Power Is Not the Same as Violence, Domination, or Determination.

Finally, Foucault is careful to distinguish power—which, as we have seen, always comes together with resistance—from what he variously calls "violence," "domination," or "determination," which are shows of overwhelming force that cannot be resisted. Whereas violence coerces, power makes its object complicit in its operation.

Discipline and Punish (1975)

In *Discipline and Punish*, Foucault analyses two regimes of power in the history of the modern West (to which, in other works, he adds at least two more, as we shall shortly see). The first is the "sovereign power" broadly characteristic of the period up to and including the Classical age.

Sovereign Power

Foucault gives the name "sovereign power" to the regime of power relations dominant in Europe until the end of the 1700s, the regime epitomized in the execution of Damiens, the attempted regicide. Despite its name, sovereign power does not always evoke an individual (the sovereign), but rather a principle. It is not necessarily about power being localized in one supreme ruler; rather, it refers to the way that power functions within a particular society, whether in terms of a monarchy, a totalitarian state, or even a democratic regime (where the locus of sovereignty is disseminated, moving from the monarch to the individual subject). The main characteristics of sovereign power can be summed up in three points: it seizes, it commands, and it takes life:

- The regime of sovereign power revolves around the notion of seizure, deduction (*prélèvement*), and appropriation

(*HS1*, 136). It appropriates the bodies of its subjects to fight in its wars, their land to provide for its reserves, and their taxes to fill its coffers.

- Second, sovereign power asserts itself through a dynamic of command and obedience. It issues orders which are to be obeyed, on pain of punishment.
- Third, and equally important, Foucault glosses sovereignty as "the right to *take* life or *let* live" (*HS1*, 138, emphasis original); the sovereign can demand of its subjects their life.

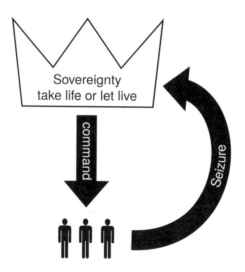

Fig. 2.4. Sovereign Power.

But why is Damiens so theatrically and excessively punished? Because the "multiple, different and irreconcilable relationships" (*LCF-PP*, 45) in a society are held together, symbolically, in the king's body, so to attack that body (whether literally, through regicide, or metaphorically, through a violation of law) is to attack the very possibility of society. It is a threat that needs to be met with overwhelming force exerted on the body of the criminal:

you attack the sovereign's body (i.e., the social order), and he or she will attack yours, only more ferociously.

Pastoral Power

Before we come to disciplinary power, the second type of power discussed at length in *Discipline and Punish*, we shall take a detour to consider another form of power, one that precedes it chronologically, the "pastoral power" that for Foucault comprises Christianity's particular contribution to the history of power relations in the West (*LCF-STP*, especially 126–33). The ancient Greek city-state functioned according to a relatively impersonal model of power in which the main concern was the healthy functioning of the city, but with the rise of the church in the West, a form of power emerged that does not primarily repress or forbid, but seeks to regulate in detail the everyday lives of believers. Foucault writes:

> Christian pastorship has introduced a game that neither the Greeks nor the Hebrews imagined. A strange game whose elements are life, death, truth, obedience, individuals, self-identity—a game which seems to have nothing to do with the game of the city surviving through the sacrifice of its citizens. (*PPC*, 70–71)

This pastoral power is intensely personal, with the shepherd (usually the local priest) holding personal responsibility for the individuals under his care, to whom those individuals are directly accountable and to whom they owe direct obedience. Pastoral power is characterized by intense, personal relationships of spiritual direction. The pastor does not wield power like a sovereign, imposing a uniform law on the undifferentiated mass of subjects through the issuing of commands backed up by punishments for disobedience, but rather shepherds each individual soul toward salvation as he hears their confession and grants them absolution.

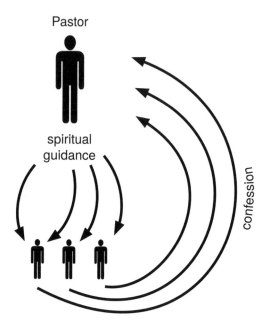

Fig. 2.5. Pastoral Power.

Disciplinary Power

Neither sovereign nor pastoral power is the dominant mode of power in the modern age. While the paradigm of sovereign power has not been dominant in our society since the Classical age, Foucault laments that it is still the model in terms of which we try to understand our contemporary situation, a thought he sums up with the now famous assertion that "the representation of power has remained under the spell of monarchy. In political thought and analysis, we still have not cut off the head of the king" (*HS1*, 88–89). What we fail to see, he argues, is that the paradigm of sovereign power has given way to the much subtler and more pervasive dynamic of "disciplinary power."

An important difference between sovereign and disciplinary power, Foucault stresses, is that whereas the former seeks to punish the body, the latter disciplines the soul. This difference reminds us of his critique of Pinel's and Tuke's "humanitarian" reforms in *History of Madness*, where he also dismissed the thesis of a growing humanitarianism over time. Disciplinary power is also different from sovereign power in that it is a "capillary" power: it does not flow from a position of sovereignty in one great torrent, but is dispersed through myriad capillaries as it "reaches into the very grain of individuals, touches their bodies and inserts itself into their actions and attitudes, their discourses, learning processes and everyday lives" (*P/K*, 39).

The idea of a strict, daily regimen, which is characteristic of disciplinary power, may have first begun in monastic orders, Foucault acknowledges (*DP*, 150), but it has become generalized through military discipline. In fact, disciplinary power takes the military parade ground as its model. The paradigm of disciplinary power, he argues, was elaborated in the seventeenth century when the invention of the rifle changed the nature of warfare. Previous to this invention, a mass army was a largely untrained rabble and "troops were used as a projectile, a wall or a fortress" (*DP*, 162). The invention of the rifle, however, meant that the soldier's skill (the ability to fire, reload, and fire again more quickly than the enemy) became highly prized. This new requirement fostered a regime of strict training and discipline, in which each movement of the body (both the bodies of individuals and the corps of soldiers) is scrutinized and honed: "The act is broken down into its elements; . . . to each movement are assigned a direction, an aptitude, a duration; their order of succession is prescribed. Time penetrates the body and with it all the meticulous controls of power" (*DP*, 152). In one of the almost off-hand, but far-reaching remarks that Foucault often throws into his analyses, he concludes that "from such

trifles, no doubt, the man of modern humanism was born"
(*DP*, 141).

Let us compare sovereign and disciplinary power a little
further:

- Whereas sovereign power seizes and appropriates, disciplinary power "draws up tables; it prescribes movements;
it imposes exercises; lastly, in order to obtain the combination of forces, it arranges 'tactics'" (*DP*, 167). In other
words, disciplinary power pays great attention to the
details of behavior and life, whereas sovereign power, to
put it bluntly, leaves people alone unless it wants something from them. For disciplinary power:

  > It was a question not of treating the body, *en masse,*
  > "wholesale," as if it were an indissociable unity, but of
  > working it "retail," individually; of exercising upon it a
  > subtle coercion, of obtaining holds upon it at the level of
  > the mechanism itself—movements, gestures, attitudes,
  > rapidity: an infinitesimal power over the active body.
  > (*DP*, 136–37)

- Whereas sovereign power operates by command, discipline works by what Foucault calls "normalization," which
is shorthand for three key moments in disciplinary power:
(1) "hierarchical observation," which makes individual
behavior visible and measurable by "eyes that must see
without being seen" (*DP*, 171); (2) "normalizing judgment," which measures and judges behavior according to
a positive norm, rather than according to whether it avoids
certain prohibitions, and (3) "examination," which com-
bines hierarchical observation and normalizing judgment
into "a surveillance that makes it possible to qualify, to
classify and to punish" (*DP*, 184).

- Whereas sovereign power has the "right to take life or let live," disciplinary power has neither the right to take life nor the right to let live. Instead, it employs a more fine-grained intervention to conform individual lives to certain standards and movements that are timed, measured, and regulated.

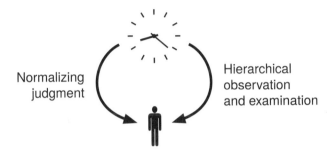

Fig. 2.6. Disciplinary Power.

Such power is not dominant only in prisons and on military parade grounds, Foucault argues. The reason he spends time discussing rifles and bed-making is that, he argues, the strict regimen of military discipline and Faucher's prison life has pervaded all of society, such that today we live in a "carceral society,"[5] in which the human sciences enlarge and perpetuate the observation and normalization of the prison, and in which institutions like factories, schools, barracks, and hospitals "all resemble prisons" (*DP*, 228).

The Panopticon

Disciplinary power characterizes the operation of one of Foucault's most famous but most misunderstood illustrations:

---

5. This term, so far as I have been able to determine, is not Foucault's own, but is frequently used in commentaries on his work.

the panopticon. This term describes a prison imagined by nine-teenth-century utilitarian philosopher Jeremy Bentham, which Foucault describes in the following way:

> At the periphery, an annular building; at the center, a tower; this tower is pierced with wide windows that open onto the inner side of the ring; the peripheric building is divided into cells, each of which extends the whole width of the building; they have two windows, one on the inside, corresponding to the windows of the tower; the other, on the outside, allows the light to cross the cell from one end to the other. All that is needed, then, is to place a supervisor in a central tower and to shut up in each cell a madman, a patient, a condemned man, a worker or a schoolboy. By the effect of backlighting, one can observe from the tower, standing out precisely against the light, the small captive shadows in the cells of the periphery. They are like so many cages, so many small theatres, in which each actor is alone, perfectly individualized and constantly visible. (*DP*, 200)

The panopticon stands as a paradigm of disciplinary power for Foucault, not primarily because its inhabitants are incarcerated, though they are, and not even because they are never sure whether they are being observed, though they are not. The "major function" of the panopticon is the way in which it causes the inmates to internalize the discipline of the guards, the way it works "to induce in the inmate a state of conscious and permanent visibility that assures the automatic functioning of power" (*DP*, 201). In other words, it works to make the inmates become their own guards. Never sure when their transgression will be observed and punished, the inmates police their own behavior and, if that internalization is complete, come to act as their own wardens without giving it a second thought: the disciplinary regime has become inseparable from who they are, essential to who they are.

The panopticon functions for Foucault like the ship of fools in *History of Madness*: his point is not that our society is full of prisons that adopt this design,[6] but that the panopticon provides a particularly pure and distilled picture of a wider reality that has been called the "panoptic society": a society characterized by generalized vigilance through self-examination with a view to self-normalization.

Biopower

In the first volume of his *History of Sexuality*, entitled *The Will to Knowledge* (1976), and in some of his lectures at the Collège de France, Foucault adds a further category of power: biopower. Biopower arises alongside disciplinary power and becomes prominent in the modern age, but whereas disciplinary power concerns itself with "the administration of bodies," biopower is the combination of disciplinary power and biopolitics. It is a set of techniques for "the calculated management of life," created to manage "the problems of birthrate, longevity, public health, housing, and migration" (*HS1*, 140). This explains why, in the nineteenth century, masturbation and hygiene (among other factors) emerge with much greater prominence than they had enjoyed in previous ages.

Whereas disciplinary power busies itself with "the body as a machine," biopower concerns itself with "the species body" (*HS1*, 139). Sovereign power treats populations only in terms of what it can extract from them and command of them: it is the power to take life or let live in the sense that it does not concern

6. The panopticon was never built as a working prison. It did, in some respects, influence the plan of La Santé in Paris and Strangeways in Manchester. To claim, as does David Macey, that it was to "provide a model" for these prisons is going too far. See David Macey, *Michel Foucault* (London: Reaktion Books, 2004), 116.

itself with the details of the lives of its subjects, but lets them live. Biopower, by stark contrast, seeks to regulate life itself: it is "a power to *foster* life or *disallow* it to the point of death" (*HS1* 138, emphasis original). "Biopolitics" is Foucault's term to describe the discourse, policies, and technologies that surround biopower. Such policies and technologies should not be understood as having been invented by a single person, but as being a consequence of power distributed throughout society in schools and hospitals, parliaments and agencies.

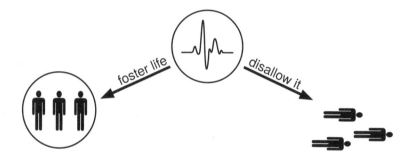

Fig. 2.7. Biopower.

Finally, we must not think of a neat historical succession from sovereign and pastoral power through disciplinary power to biopower. The different forms function together in society, and what changes over time is "the dominant characteristic, or more exactly, the system of correlation" between them (*LCF-STP*, 8).

The Normative Critique

One important question raised by the turn to more overtly political themes in Foucault's genealogies is to what extent his work lends itself to normative conclusions. The stories Foucault is telling describe the presence of different concepts and behaviors at different historical moments, but do not in themselves suggest which—if any—of these concepts or behaviors are to be preferred over others. Is sovereign power better than disciplinary power? Is biopower the worst of the lot or an improvement on what went before? This lack of normativity has drawn the ire of some commentators and provoked puzzlement in many more. Nancy Fraser provides an exemplary articulation of this critique when she asks, "Why is struggle preferable to submission? Why ought domination to be resisted? Only with the introduction of normative notions could he begin to tell us what is wrong with the modern power/knowledge regime and why we ought to oppose it."[7] How is the power that is exerted in resisting normalization any different from the power of that normalization? How, to put it most crassly, do you decide between "good power" and "bad power"? Commentators sympathetic to Foucault are often hesitant in their defense of him on this point. Todd May, for example, ventures that "these are difficult questions, ones that Foucault's writings do not address, except perhaps to invoke the term 'intolerable' with regard to particular practices or power arrangements."[8]

In seeking to elaborate a Foucauldian response, it behooves us to understand what the problem is. The problem is not that Foucault himself is not politically committed. His political commitments were manifested eloquently by his interventions on behalf of Vietnamese boat people in the late 1970s and early 1980s, his involvement in the Groupe d'information sur les prisons (Prisons Information Group) from 1971 to 1972, his vocal support of the Solidarity movement in Poland, and his support for the Iranian Revolution of 1979. The problem is whether or not that commitment can find any justification or basis in his writings.

7. Nancy Fraser, *Unruly Practices* (Cambridge: Polity Press, 1989), 29.
8. May, *The Philosophy of Foucault*, 123.

Perhaps the best place to start, in responding to this problem, is to point out that Foucault does not pretend to be providing a justification for a particular political position. He maintains that "there is always something ludicrous in philosophical discourse, when it tries, from the outside, to dictate to others, to tell them where their truth is and how to find it" (*HS2*, 9). Short of handing down the sort of universal judgments he condemns here, however, he is more than willing to offer reasons for the positions that he takes. Nevertheless, he always does so in a local and particular way. To do anything else, let us remember, would be to undermine his own rejection of anthropological universals and the Hegelian-Marxist view of history as controlled by unchanging norms and a fixed destiny. To lay down ethical or political norms would, in short, be to totalize and to limit the proliferation of micro-solutions and micro-alternatives that characterize his thought on everything from madness through power to sexuality:

> If I don't ever say what must be done, it isn't because I believe that there's nothing to be done; on the contrary, it is because I think that there are a thousand things to do, to invent, to forge, on the part of those who, recognizing the relations of power in which they're implicated, have decided to resist or escape them. (*LCF-WK*, 237)

To be sure, this does not resolve the normative question to everyone's satisfaction, and it does not demonstrate why "resistance" and "escape" are to be desired above conformity and normalization in the first place, but it does move the debate on from (falsely) asserting that there are no normative commitments in Foucault's work.

3

ETHICS AND IDENTITY

Have you heard the old joke about a Presbyterian shipwrecked on a desert island?[1] He lives there in complete isolation for years on end before, one day, a passing ship happens to notice him and drops anchor to rescue this religious Robinson Crusoe. Arriving ashore, the rescue party is puzzled to see that the castaway has built two churches next to each other on the shore. Asked why he has constructed two such edifices, the Presbyterian replies, "O you see, this one here is the church I go to. And that one next to it, that's the church I'd never dream of going to: I don't like the way they do things there."

Please allow me now to ruin this joke for you (if indeed there is anything to ruin). The castaway neatly illustrates two aspects of Foucault's work on sexuality that I shall spend most of this chapter exploring. The first has to do with his building the churches in the first place. Before the castaway sets to work on the island, neither of the churches exists. In fact, they are both built for the

---

1. The joke is told in many forms. Insert the religious or political nomenclature of your choice.

express purpose that one of them may be positively valued and the other negatively valued. Similarly, for Foucault, sexuality (heterosexuality, homosexuality, and other possible sexualities) is, like almost everything else, an effect of power relations and not an anthropological universal. To put it crudely, sexuality is "made," rather than simply "found," and, as we shall hear Foucault explain shortly, it is made with particular ends in view. Second, the preference for one church over another is sustained by a discourse: "I don't like the way they do things there." In order to justify his decision to frequent one church rather than the other, the castaway is obliged to classify and enumerate the practices of the disfavored church (one might imagine him complaining about the pews, the hymns, and the voice of the preacher). In a similar way, valuing different sexualities positively and negatively requires the careful classification and analysis of sexual practices, in order that it may be clearly understood what is normal and abnormal.

In this chapter, we shall examine what Foucault has to say about sexuality in general and Victorian sexuality in particular. This will take us into the work of the 1980s, his final period, commonly known as "ethical," following on from the "archaeological" (1960s) and "genealogical" (1970s) periods. For Foucault, the word "ethics" describes the relation of the self to itself, the self-formation that subjects a body to a particular regime or set of rules. Modern attitudes toward sex and sexuality, he argues, owe a great debt to Christianity, and so, in seeking to understand Foucault's work on sex and identity, we shall begin with an overview of what he has to say about the Christian religion.

Foucault on Christianity

Consonant with his examination of forms of behavior in *History of Madness* and *Discipline and Punish*, Foucault's interest is not in Christian theology, but in Christian practice. We will not come across Foucault discussing theories of the atonement or interpretations of Genesis; his analysis focuses on power relations in Christian communities and the formation of the Christian self through practices of confession and renunciation.

Confession

Let us begin our investigation of confession by returning to the discussion of pastoral power in the previous chapter. Central to the forms of behavior that enable and support pastoral power is regular, personal confession to a priest. Confession plays a crucial role, both in Foucault's account of Christianity and in his account of sexuality, so it is worth taking a little time to explain how he understands it. Originating in the monasteries of the fourth and fifth centuries, the practice of rigorous self-examination and confession of sin to a spiritual director subsequently spread to the laity and was formalized and mandated in the Fourth Lateran Council of 1215. As the practice developed into the Reformation period, it became a more rigorous self-examination at the level of one's deepest desires, its aim being to make clear not what one has done, but who one is. Furthermore, the way that the self comes to light in confession is through language. It is by speaking about myself that I come to learn who I am, as I transform my desire into discourse (*HS1*, 21). This dynamic is central to Foucault's understanding of Christianity:

> Christianity is not only a salvation religion, it's a confessional religion. . . . Each person has the duty to know who he is, that is, to try to know what is happening inside him, to acknowledge faults, to recognize temptations, to locate desires, and everyone is obliged to disclose these things either to God or to others in the community and hence to bear public or private witness against oneself. (*EW1-EST*, 242)

Furthermore, the practice of confession is not simply passive; it serves to construct the self that is confessed: in confessing my deepest desires, I not only voice who I am; I become who I am. Confession is "nothing less than the shaping of the self" (*EW1-EST*, 212).

This understanding of confession both relies on and cultivates a particular concept of the self, and it does so in three important ways. First, it implies that there is a truth about the self—a "real me," if you like—and that this deepest truth about the self is its desires: "Tell me what you desire and I will tell you what you are."[2] Second, it assumes that this truth is hidden, requiring a diligent work of interpretation to bring it to light, just like an obscure work of literature (*EW1-EST*, 95–106). This requires the believer to engage in a "permanent hermeneutics of oneself" (*EW1-EST*, 182), a constant contemplation and careful interpretation of one's hidden desires. Third, confession serves to normalize the self. It operates, not primarily according to the permitted/forbidden logic of sovereign power, but in terms of the normal/abnormal dyad of disciplinary power.

Finally, the end goal of confession is the renunciation of the desires that have been confessed. Indeed, renunciation is a major theme in Foucault's understanding of Christianity. The Christian life is a struggle in which ethical progress can only come through renouncing pleasure: "You cannot disclose without renouncing.... Throughout Christianity there is a correlation between disclosure of the self, dramatic or verbalized, and the renunciation of self" (*EW1-EST*, 249). This renunciation also embraces the Christian's relationship to his or her pastor, a relationship which requires "complete subordination" (*LCF-STP*, 162, 175) and a giving of the self over to the purposes of God and his earthly representative.

---

2. The phrase is not Foucault's own, but comes from David Macey, *Michel Foucault* (London: Reaktion Books, 2004), 118, 125.

The Confessing Society

Beginning in the sixteenth century, Foucault argues, this Christian practice of confession began to permeate the whole of society. This puts him in conflict with the traditional "secularization thesis," according to which the West has seen a gradual decline in religious practice in the modern era. For Foucault, the secularization thesis could not be further from the truth, and the sixteenth century "is not characterized by the beginning of de-Christianization, but rather, as a number of historians have shown, by a phase of in-depth Christianization" (*LCF-A*, 177). Day-to-day life in the modern age requires disclosure of the smallest details of existence, so that practices and even thoughts can be observed and normalized. This makes of society as a whole an "unrelenting system of confession" (*HS1*, 61). For Foucault, this mania for confession has today become all-pervasive:

> Confession has spread its effects far and wide. It plays a part in justice, medicine, education, family relationships, and love relations, in the most ordinary affairs of everyday life, and in the most solemn rites; one confesses one's crimes, one's sins, one's thoughts and desires, one's illnesses and troubles; one goes about telling, with the greatest precision, whatever is most difficult to tell. The most defenseless tenderness and the bloodiest of powers have a similar need of confession. Western man has become a confessing animal. (*HS1*, 59)

Sara Mills muses that this pattern of confession "can be seen in a wide range of practices today, ranging from therapeutic counselling, testimonia/autobiographical writing and reality-TV and in gay and lesbian 'coming out.'"[3] We might add that the compulsive use of social media closely resembles a pervasive

3. Sara Mills, *Michel Foucault* (London: Routledge, 2003), 86.

public confession of one's desires on a range of subjects, and the ability to comment on or "like" these confessions can be seen as a moment of normalizing judgment. J. Joyce Schuld, for her part, argues that the dynamic of confessor and confessee is present throughout modern society:

> It makes its presence felt in even the most innocuous places: at cosmetic counters with their white lab-coated "clinicians," in the self-help section of bookstores, in gymnasiums with their personal trainers and videos, and the well-intended advice of family, friends, and counsellors.[4]

These confessors, to be sure, do not shepherd us on the road from sin to salvation; they lead us on a more worldly path of redemption to "health, well-being (that is, sufficient wealth, standard of living), security, protection against accidents" (*EW3-P*, 334).

While this confessional imperative operates in all areas of life, it is most acute in the domain of sexual desire, with the effect that "between each of us and our sex, the West has placed a never-ending demand for truth" (*HS1*, 77): we must speak the truth of who we are sexually. To conclude this brief survey of confession in its Christian and modern contexts, we can see that, in the same way that Foucault argued in *Discipline and Punish* that we live in a carceral society, in the first volume of his *History of Sexuality* the claim is that we have become "a singularly confessing society" (*HS1*, 59) and that this generalized practice of confession is a key dynamic in the creation of what he calls the "modern soul" (*DP*, 23).

---

4. J. Joyce Schuld, *Foucault and Augustine: Reconsidering Power and Love* (Notre Dame, IN: Notre Dame University Press, 2003), 151–52.

The Will to Knowledge: The History
of Sexuality, Volume 1 (1976)

This survey of Foucault's reconstruction of the practice of confession and its spread throughout society sets the stage for the first volume of his *History of Sexuality*, his second great genealogical text after *Discipline and Punish*. This is one of Foucault's most widely read works, and is recognized as a seminal text in gay and lesbian studies, as well as in queer theory. The book begins with a study of sexuality in the Victorian age.

The Repressive Hypothesis

Here is a quick experiment: what words first come to mind when you hear the phrase "the Victorians and sex"? Prudery? Puritanism? Repression? Silence? Unless you have read Foucault, it is likely that words like these will be high on your list. "Victorian" has practically become a byword for sexual repression today: we all know that the Victorians did not talk about sex. Since those dark, puritanical days however—so the usual story goes—we have been sexually "liberated" through a "revolution" which leaves us free to express ourselves. In the first volume of his *History of Sexuality*, Foucault argues passionately that this is a distortion of the truth: the Victorians talked more about sex than previous generations, not less, and the notion that we are now sexually liberated is just as much a misunderstanding as the claim that Pinel and Tuke unproblematically emancipated the mad or that humanitarian progress exhaustively accounts for the end of public torture.

In the first volume of his *History of Sexuality*, Foucault calls this likely story of Victorian sexuality the "repressive hypothesis." His problem with the repressive hypothesis is not its claim that talk of sex was repressed in the Victorian era, but its implication that this repression tells the whole story of nineteenth-century attitudes toward sexuality. He insists that there was a veritable "discursive explosion" around sexuality that ran alongside and interacted with this repression, aimed at the biopolitical regulation and normalization of groups that until that point had not been the sustained object of discourse. Foucault focuses on four such groups: the hysterical woman, the masturbating child, the perverse adult, and the Malthusian couple.[5] "It was time," he writes, "for all these figures, scarcely noticed in the past, to step forward and speak, to make the difficult confession of what they were" (*HS1*, 39). For that to happen, the Victorian age developed a sophisticated "apparatus for producing an ever greater quantity of discourse about sex" (*HS1*, 23), an apparatus that proliferated sex-talk and produced "a centrifugal movement with respect to heterosexual monogamy" (*HS1*, 38).

Just as Foucault seeks to demonstrate that there was more to the Victorians than repression, he also insists that there was more to the twentieth-century sexual revolution than liberation from a restrictive past. It follows from Foucault's tracing of generalized confession in the modern world that—contrary to what most people assume—the sexual revolution of the 1960s was by no means a rejection of the religious, but rather a secularized practice of religious confession. It reinforced and gave new vigor to the quintessentially religious notions that sexual desire is the deepest truth of the individual and that this desire needs to be spoken. There is a direct and unbroken line of continuity between Christian confession and the twentieth-century discourse of sexual liberation.

Sexuality Is Constructed by Its Discourse

We have seen that the modern discourse around homosexuality first arose as the combination of (1) a nineteenth-century

---

5. Named after the scholar Thomas Robert Malthus (1766–1834), the Malthusian couple describes the couple whose reproductive potential is regulated in order to avoid what Malthus saw as the dangers of overpopulation.

biopolitical bid to catalogue and label the various sexual practices that threatened the smooth regulation of the population,
and (2) Christian practices of confessing one's deepest desires as
a way to discover who one really is. Remember, though, that in
Foucault's understanding of the Christian confessional, confession does not merely register the truth of a desiring self that was
waiting to be discovered, but actively constructs that self in the
practice of confession. The same dynamic is at play, he argues, in
the modern discourse of sexuality. We tend to assume that sex is
the object of the discourse of sexuality, waiting out there in the
world to be discovered and labelled with the appropriate terms.
The relation, Foucault insists, is in fact quite the reverse: sex is
the product of the discourse of sexuality. What does Foucault
mean by this? He explains his position in the following way: In
the nineteenth century

> the notion of "sex" made it possible to group together, in an
> artificial unity, anatomical elements, biological functions,
> conducts, sensations, pleasures; and it enabled one to make
> use of this fictitious unity as a causal principle, an omnipresent
> meaning, a secret to be discovered everywhere. (*HS1*, 154)

This new category of "sexuality" can then be read back into
the phenomena that it originally grouped together, justifying
itself through its reverse-engineered explanatory power. But we
must be careful: Foucault is not singling sexuality out for special
treatment here. When he claims that "homosexuality is a notion
that dates from the nineteenth century, and thus . . . is a recent
category" (GS, 386), he is not singling out his own homosexuality for special treatment or suggesting anything qualitatively
different from his judgment of all historical realities, from
madness through forms of punishment to the understanding
of disease: just like everything else (including heterosexuality

and "sexuality" in general), homosexuality is no "anthropological universal." Nor is he suggesting, of course, that same-sex intercourse dates only from the nineteenth century. What he is arguing is that this behavior had a very different meaning prior to the Victorian discursive explosion. From the ancient world until the eighteenth century, he argues, same-sex intercourse was seen in terms of the difference between the active and the passive partner or as an expression of libertinage. What dates from the nineteenth century is the idea that homosexual practice is an expression of the deepest identity of the persons involved: an act (sodomy) is replaced with an identity (homosexuality). In Foucault's own words, "the homosexual was now a species" (*HS1*, 43). Indeed, so deep and intimate is the relationship between sexuality and identity that Foucault can write of the emergence of sexuality in the nineteenth and twentieth centuries in religious terms:

> We expect our intelligibility to come from what was for many centuries thought of as madness, . . . our identity from what was perceived as a nameless urge. Hence the importance we ascribe to it, the reverential fear with which we surround it, the care we take to know it. Hence the fact that over the centuries it has become more important to us than our soul. (*HS1*, 156)

This is not only an ascription of religious importance to sexuality; it is the culmination of an unbroken development of the Christian practice of confession.

An Ethic of Self-Transformation

Foucault's understanding of sexuality is not merely descriptive. It is at the heart of an ethic of self-transformation that emerges most clearly in his work of the 1980s and that has personal, social, and political dimensions. This ethic of self-transformation starts from the position that there is no deep truth of the individual, no essence waiting to be discovered and named: sex is not the object of the discourse of sexuality, but its product. In fact, the very idea that I can tell "the truth" about myself is itself a symptom of being normalized: "If I tell the truth about myself . . . it is in part that I am constituted as a subject across a number of power relations which are exerted over me and which I exert over others" (*EW2-AME*, 452). Rather than seeking in vain to tell the deep and hidden truths about ourselves, we ought to take upon ourselves the responsibility of creating our identity in general and our sexuality in particular.

This can be seen in the appropriation by homosexuals of the language of sexual perversion originally invented to label them for biopolitical ends. What began as a discourse of control and normalization became a language of affirmation, for once homosexuality had been given a status as a perversion within nineteenth-century discourse, it "began to speak on its behalf, to demand that its legitimacy or 'naturality' be acknowledged" (*HS1*, 101). Rather than refusing the Victorian pathologizing discourse, by

> taking such discourses literally, and thereby turning them around, we see responses arising in the form of defiance: "All right, we are the same as you, by nature sick or perverse, whichever you want. And so if we are, let us be so, and if you want to know what we are, we can tell you better than you can."
> (*PPC*, 115)

The adoption of this language is not to be understood as the admission that sexuality is, after all, the essence of the "true self." The aim is not recognition but creative self-fashioning in the context of an ethic of self-transformation. Sexuality is not a discovery but an invention, for "we don't have to discover that we are homosexuals . . . we have to create a gay life" (*EW1-EST,* 163).

Furthermore, this gay life is not simply a question of sexual practices. Foucault sees the stakes of self-transformation as much broader than sexual preference. It is a way of being in the world:

> Is it possible to create a homosexual mode of life? This notion of mode of life seems important to me. . . . It seems to me that a way of life can yield a culture and an ethics. To be "gay," I think, is not to identify with the psychological traits and the visible marks of the homosexual, but to try to define and develop a way of life. (*EW1-EST*, 137–38)

To be gay in this way is not to "come out" in the sense of publicly acknowledging the truth of one's deepest desires; it is to see the gay lifestyle as something to be desired and as a political stance with the intention of creating a different sort of society. It does not confine and label the body either as "homosexual" or "heterosexual," but turns the body into "a place for the production of extraordinarily polymorphous pleasures, detached from the valorization of sex" (GS, 396–97).

Cultivating a gay lifestyle stands in relation to the creation of the modern self, for Foucault, as do spiritual exercises to the forming of the medieval Christian self: it is an askesis—an "exercise of oneself in the activity of thought" (*HS2*, 9) by which "we create ourselves as a work of art" (*FR*, 351)—that lies at the heart of a practice of self-mastery and self-creation. Foucault does not argue that the implications of this creative lifestyle lie merely on the personal or interpersonal level; it provides an opportunity, not only to create the individual, but to recreate society:

> Homosexuality is a historic occasion to reopen affective and relational virtualities, not so much through the intrinsic

qualities of the homosexual, but because the "slantwise" position of the latter, as it were, the diagonal lines he can lay out in the social fabric allow these virtualities to come to light. (*EW1-EST*, 138)

Sex serves to transform the individual and society, not only by offering nontraditional, "off-center" identities and practices, but also as one mode of what, in a 1978 interview with Duccio Trombadori, Foucault calls "limit-experience." He describes the notion of "limit-experience" as the attempt in writers like Friedrich Nietzsche, Georges Bataille, and Maurice Blanchot "to reach that point of life which lies as close as possible to the impossibility of living, which lies at the limit or extreme" (*RM*, 27). Such experiences transgress accepted codes of behavior in any number of ways; examples include madness, sadomasochism, crime, death, torture, and violence. Whereas customary understandings of "experience"[6] attempt "to grasp the significance of daily experience in order to reaffirm the fundamental character of the subject, of the self," the limit-experience has quite the opposite effect. Rather than consolidating and affirming the subject, it has "the task of 'tearing' the subject from itself in such a way that it is no longer the subject as such, or that it is completely 'other' than itself so that it may arrive at its annihilation, its dissociation" (*RM*, 31). For Bataille, for example, "the whole business of eroticism is to destroy the self-contained character of the participators as they are in their normal lives."[7]

If we return to the normalized subject of disciplinary power, for instance, limit-experiences disturb the careful control and disciplining of the body upon which such a subject relies:

6. Foucault refers specifically in the interview to the phenomenological tradition of Edmund Husserl and Martin Heidegger.

7. Georges Bataille, *Eroticism: Death and Sensuality*, trans. Mary Dalwood (San Francisco: City Lights, 1986), 17.

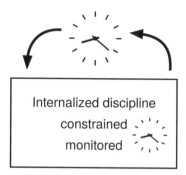

Fig. 3.1. The Normalized Subject.

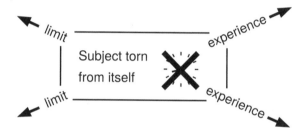

Fig. 3.2. The limit-experience destabilizes the normalized subject.

The value of limit-experience is that, as it "wrenches the subject from itself" (*EW3-P*, 241), it prevents the subject from ossifying into a stagnant, unchanging set of repeated thoughts and behaviors, opening it up to self-transformation. Indeed, it is this Nietzschean, Bataillian, and Blanchotian notion that "explains the fact that however boring, however erudite my books may be, I've always conceived of them as direct experiences aimed at pulling myself free of myself, at preventing me from being the same" (*EW3-P*, 241–42).

Foucault against the Emancipation Narrative?

Foucault's advocacy for the creative invention of gay forms of life, rather than for the discovery of some deep, inner sexual truth of the self, means that he is opposed—counterintuitively for many who have only a superficial acquaintance with his work— to the emancipation narrative that drives much twentieth- and twenty-first-century discourse and policy on sexual matters. The emancipation narrative, rather like the repressive hypothesis, claims that we just need to be liberated in our sexual practices in order to enjoy what we might call "your best sex now." Freedom, however, is emphatically not the antithesis of power for Foucault, and liberation itself "opens up new relationships of power, which have to be controlled by practices of liberty" (ECS, 4). The move from oppression to liberation is in fact the transition from one regime of control to another.

One problem Foucault has with the emancipation narrative is that it is at home with Hegelian-Marxian totalizing philosophies of history, seeing the liberation of humanity from everything that constrains it as the primary goal and meaning of history. A second problem that makes Foucault "somewhat suspicious of the notion of liberation" (*EW1-EST*, 282) is that it assumes there to be an unchanging, essential human nature that needs to be freed from the forces that constrain it, whereas Foucault himself, as we have seen above (in chapter 2, under the heading "The subject is constituted as a reciprocal interplay of power and resistance"), claims that the subject is constituted by power in the first place. The very idea of a sexual human nature that needs to be liberated from oppression would invalidate Foucault's ethic of creative self-transformation.

Nevertheless—and this is less frequently commented on in the secondary literature than his rejection of the emancipation narrative—Foucault does propound a form of emancipation: not

of truth from power, but of truth-power from control by conglom-
erate entities like the state and large corporations. There is a bias
for the individual over the state in comments such as "It's not a
matter of emancipating truth from every system of power (which
would be a chimera, for truth is already power) but of detaching
the power of truth from the forms of hegemony" (*EW3-P*, 133).
It makes no sense to talk of liberating the individual from power
as such, but Foucault still wants us to be liberated from normalizing subjectivations in order to be able to perform creative self-
transformation.

4

CONCLUSION OF PART 1 AND INTERLUDE: FOUCAULT AND THE THEOLOGIANS

To conclude this first half of the book, let us consider how we might draw together our analysis of Foucault's work through its archaeological, genealogical, and ethical phases. Here are five summary points:

- Foucault is not writing history for history's sake, but a "history of the present" (*DP*, 31) that enables us to understand ourselves better.
- He wants to write histories of the present because he judges certain contemporary practices—those related to disciplinary power and biopower, seeking to regulate and normalize human life—as "intolerable."[1]

1. For example, his comments on the death sentence in "Pompidou's two deaths":

   That [the guillotine] still exists, forms part of our institutions, convokes around its ceremony the magistracy, the Church, the armed police, and, in the shadows, the president of the republic—in short, all the powers that

- He writes histories of the present with the important aim (among others) of disturbing convention and the sense that things have always been, and must always be, as they currently are. His history "deprives the self of the reassuring stability of life and nature, and it will not permit itself to be transported by a voiceless obstinacy toward a millennial ending" (*EW2-AME*, 380).
- The aim of this unsettling is to introduce creativity, novelty, and difference: "The object was to learn to what extent the effort to think one's own history can free thought from what it silently thinks, and so enable it to think differently" (*HS2*, 9), or again: "My role . . . is to show people that they are much freer than they feel" (*TPS*, 10).
- To condense this trajectory into one necessarily but unpardonably brief thought, we might conclude that Foucault's work is driven by the conviction that "the main interest in life is to become someone else that you were not at the beginning. . . . The game is worthwhile insofar as we don't know what will be the end" (*TPS*, 9).

Interlude: Foucault and the Theologians

Much has been written on the implications of Foucault's thought for theology and religious practice, from a broad range of theological perspectives. In this brief interlude, I can do no more than give a flavor of the diversity of ways in which his thought has been brought into conversation with theology and theological themes.

Jonathan Tran's *Foucault and Theology*, in Bloomsbury's Philosophy and Theology series, aims not to consider how the

---

be. There is something about it that is physically and politically intolerable. (*EW3-P*, 418)

Frenchman's work "can be considered 'theological'," but rather to explore how "Foucault helps Christians think about Christian faithfulness,"[2] particularly through his understanding of power. He argues that Foucault offers hope in an age of despair, a hope which he seeks to set to a Christian rhythm. Drawing a link between Foucauldian askesis and Christian discipleship, he argues that both are expressions of a care of the self, a term understood to mean "the self's ability to tell its own story, to both be determined by and determine the meaning of its existence."[3] What is at stake in any such use of Foucault for Tran is whether he weds himself to a Nietzschean ontology. Tran concludes that he does not, and that therefore he is usable by Christians. It seems to me that Tran is too quick to assimilate power relations in Foucault to power in Christian theology and the Bible. As I will explain below, the Bible has a distinctive way of thinking about power that, to my mind at least, Tran underplays.

J. Joyce Schuld's *Foucault and Augustine* draws a number of persuasive links between its two eponymous subjects: they both critique discourses which, in their day, were self-evident,[4] they share the same sort of "subversive hope,"[5] and Augustine's paradigm of considering relationships through the lens of love bears comparison and highlights fruitful contrasts with power relations in Foucault's work. Her stance is discerning and broadly balanced, resolving to the position that "Foucault ought to be read as providing a highly nuanced critique of distinct segments of the contemporary social environment that Christians can then examine with a different sort of attentiveness that is guided by a

2. Jonathan Tran, *Foucault and Theology* (London: Bloomsbury, 2011), 3.

3. Ibid., 2.

4. J. Joyce Schuld, *Foucault and Augustine: Reconsidering Power and Love* (Notre Dame, IN: Notre Dame University Press, 2003), 159.

5. Ibid., 3–4.

different set of presuppositions."[6] Foucault's questioning of contemporary assumptions poses no threat to Christian discourses
and practices for Schuld, and the Frenchman "can creatively crit-
icize and enrich an Augustinian standpoint, thereby making it
better suited to detecting and responding to the shifting risks of
a post-modern world."[7]

In *Foucault and Religion: Spiritual Corporality and Political
Spirituality*, Jeremy Carrette contends that "after Foucault 'religion' is taken out of its privileged realm and brought into the
body politic and into the heart of culture,"[8] specifically in terms
of what he sees as two moments in Foucault's work which he
calls "spiritual corporality" and "political spirituality." As Carrette
rightly notes, "this reading of religion will always be difficult to
anyone hoping to use Foucault to support traditional religious
belief and practice."[9]

For James Bernauer—who, along with Carrette, is perhaps
the most respected scholar on religion within Foucault studies—Foucault is something of a negative theologian. If Carrette
uses Foucault to make theology political, then Bernauer uses him
to make politics theological. In *Michel Foucault's Force of Flight:
Toward an Ethics for Thought*, Bernauer gives a detailed account
of Foucault's engagement with theology (often drawing on his
lesser-read articles and interviews), and argues that Foucault's
politically motivated dissolution of the disciplinary subject is a
"negative anthropology" that blossoms into a "negative theology," given that "its flight from man is an escape from yet another
conceptualization of the Absolute."[10]

6. Ibid., 18.
7. Ibid., 8.
8. Jeremy Carrette, *Foucault and Religion* (London: Routledge, 2002), xi.
9. Ibid.
10. James W. Bernauer, *Michel Foucault's Force of Flight: Toward an Ethics for
Thought* (New York: Humanity Books, 2000), 178.

In *Theology and Social Theory*, John Milbank offers the most negative assessment of Foucault's work in this brief survey, grouping him together with Nietzsche, Heidegger, Deleuze, Lyotard, and Derrida as "elaborations of a single nihilistic philosophy."[11] Judging Foucault's histories to be politically motivated, Milbank argues that "genealogy is not an interpretation, but a new 'joyfully' nihilistic form of positivism which explains every cultural meaning-complex as a particular strategy or ruse of power."[12] This is half right. Foucault is quite ready to agree that he is not writing traditional history of the "just the facts, ma'am" variety, but, as I have shown above, his emphasis on the ubiquity of power relations is not the end of his analysis, but a means to the end of a politics of (self-)transformation that emerges most clearly in his later ethical work. Milbank rightly challenges Foucault's interpretation—as I will also do below— of Christianity as a religion of *ressentiment* (Nietzsche's term for a vengeful and petty-minded resentment of the strong by the weak) and asceticism, arguing that "nihilism cannot 'position' Christianity in its genealogy, in a way that amounts to more than interpretation" and therefore cannot adequately argue for its own "reading of every event as an event of warfare."[13] What we can learn from Foucault, Milbank concludes, is that the modern state took the form of a church, exercising pastoral power and "concentrating on the minute regulation of bodies in time and space."[14]

In his brief treatment of Foucault in *Who's Afraid of Postmodernism?* James K. A. Smith seeks to "take Foucault to church," showing how his thought can be helpful to Christians.

11. John Milbank, *Theology and Social Theory: Beyond Secular Reason*, 2nd ed. (Oxford: Blackwell, 2006), 278.

12. Ibid., 262.

13. Ibid., 295. See also 289–91.

14. Ibid., 440.

There is a grain of truth in Smith's numbering of Foucault among Enlightenment thinkers of liberation (he also mentions Kant and Marx),[15] but it would be easy to be misled into thinking that Foucault is closer to the two Germans than he in fact is. Smith goes too far when he says that Foucault, as a liberal, is opposed "to domination and control as such."[16] As we have seen, Foucault's problems with Kant and Marx, not least in their notions of liberation,[17] are profound, and Foucault fully recognizes that liberation itself is a form of control. What Smith seems to value most in Foucault's work is the notion of disciplinary power:

> Foucault is absolutely right in his analysis of the way in which mechanisms of discipline serve to form individuals, but he is wrong to cast all such discipline and formation in a negative light. In other words, Christians should understand discipline positively. . . . By rejecting Foucault's liberal Enlightenment commitments, but appropriating his analyses of the role of discipline in formation, we can almost turn Foucault's project on its head.[18]

Without further clarification it is hard, however, to see how disciplinary techniques can be abstracted from their Foucauldian context in the rise of capitalism and the cult of efficiency in order to be transplanted into the context of Christian community

15. "The very goal of Enlightenment is liberation, which is why both Kant and Marx are Enlightenment thinkers. And insofar as Foucault's work feeds into just such impulses, it is hard not to see a libertarian streak in his descriptions" (James K. A. Smith, *Who's Afraid of Postmodernism? Taking Derrida, Lyotard, and Foucault to Church* [Grand Rapids: Baker Academic, 2006], 98).

16. Ibid., 102.

17. For Foucault's views on Kant's notion of liberation in his famous *sapere aude* ("dare to know"), see Michel Foucault, "What Is Enlightenment?" (*EW1-EST*, 303–19).

18. Smith, *Who's Afraid of Postmodernism?*, 99.

without reducing Foucault's analysis to the banal (and no longer distinctively Foucauldian) point that we are formed through our behaviors and habits, not just our beliefs.

PART 2

INTRODUCING THE CRUCIFORM "GREAT REVERSAL"

In this second part of the book, we turn to reflect on Foucault in the light of a Reformed understanding of the Bible. My aim is to bring Foucault and the Bible themselves, as far as I can, into direct conversation, rather than adding yet one more layer of commentary to an already gargantuan palimpsest. Positively stated, my aim in this second part of the book is to engage Foucault's thought with biblical motifs and a biblical way of thinking, drawing on secondary texts at those points where they directly help to accomplish this central task. My primary concern is neither exclusively to seek out those points of affinity that may exist between Foucault and the Bible, nor only to draw clearly the areas of disagreement, though I hope that both of these will emerge in the course of the discussion below. My intention is, in the first instance, to accord to the Bible the same privilege I have extended to Foucault: to let it set out an understanding of history, power, and identity in its own terms, and then to bring this biblical account into conversation with Foucault's ideas by exploring common concerns or problems that they both seek to address.

This approach of mine will no doubt be problematic in the eyes of some. For example, in one of the very few comparative philosophical treatments of the theme of power in Foucault and the apostle Paul, Elizabeth A. Castelli dismisses the sort of approach I am attempting here.[1] Castelli admits the attractiveness of the idea that "texts should be 'allowed to speak for themselves,'" but dismisses it as a utopian fancy, according to which "texts exist in a benign, neutral free market which, when left to its own devices, merely allows the best ideas to win out."[2] My own reading rejects the dichotomy between Castelli's utopian free market and her own approach of interrogating "first-century texts through the lens of twentieth-century theories and concerns,"[3] which we might think of, to extend her own metaphor, as a market loaded with trade barriers and rigged for exploitation. I am guided by the principle of *audi alteram partem* (listen to the other side), which—like Oscar Wilde's characterization of truth—is rarely pure and never simple, but is not, for all that, utopian or fanciful. For Castelli, Foucault is the subject and Paul is the object of analysis. I want to avoid this hierarchy (or its inverse) by letting each party speak for itself before trying to initiate a conversation between them. I do not claim to have done so perfectly, but I do believe that this approach is worthwhile.

All of this may well result in there being far too much theology here for philosophers and far too much philosophy for theologians. So be it. My reason for proceeding in this way is that I do not believe there can be a meaningful exchange between

---

1. Elizabeth E. Castelli, "Interpretations of Power in 1 Corinthians," *Semeia* 54 (1991): 197–222.

2. Ibid., 199.

3. Ibid.

Foucault and the Bible under the banner of *audi alteram partem* without first letting each party set out its own stall in its own way, and only then inviting them both to a common marketplace of ideas. The reader will have to judge for himself or herself whether this approach is vindicated in the analyses that follow.

Introducing the Cruciform "Great Reversal"

There would doubtless be a great many ways in which to engage with Foucault's thought from a biblical point of view, but I have decided to privilege one biblical motif in these pages. It is a recurring biblical "move" (we could also call it a recurring "shape of biblical thought") that is known among theologians by a number of different terms including the "theology of paradox,"[4] the "theology of the cross," or the "great reversal,"[5] to which I will add my own terms below: "biblical subversion," "biblical nonlinearity," and "v-shaped and x-shaped biblical thinking." I will move between these different terms in the analyses that follow in order to draw on the varying nuances and emphases of each one, but it is important to realize that I am treating them as different facets of the same biblical diamond.

The move I am describing is present throughout the Bible. It is the dynamic whereby God subverts worldly expectations of wisdom and power by choosing the weak, foolish, or powerless to accomplish his purposes. It is the dynamic according to which:

4. Though this term is commonly used to refer more broadly to the thought of theologians like Søren Kierkegaard and Karl Barth, it also refers to a prominent feature of Luther's thought exemplified in his description of "theologians of the cross," discussed below. In these pages, I intend the term not in its full Barthian sense, but as evoking the biblical pattern of God's words and actions running athwart commonsense human expectations.

5. See for example Allen Verhey, *The Great Reversal: Ethics and the New Testament* (Grand Rapids: Eerdmans, 1984).

- Yahweh chooses the octogenarian idol worshipper Abraham and his barren wife Sarah to be "the father of a multitude of nations" (Gen. 17:5).
- It is not Abraham's firstborn Ishmael who will be in the line of the promise, but "through Isaac shall your offspring be named" (Gen. 21:12).
- Jacob, the younger son of Isaac, inherits in the place of Esau, the firstborn (Gen. 27).
- Moses, the abandoned orphan with a speech impediment, rescues his people from Pharaoh (Ex. 14).
- David, the youngest of his brothers and initially over-looked even by the prophet Samuel (1 Sam. 16), is the great king of God's people who leads them to victory and in whose line the Messiah will be born, not the rugged Saul who looks much more the part.
- Ruth the destitute Moabite foreigner (Ruth 1:3–5) is grafted into the family line of God's Messiah (Matt. 1:5).
- Isaiah prophesies that God will bring low the rich and exalt the poor (Isa. 29:16–21).
- The newly pregnant Mary, a vulnerable, unmarried girl probably from an artisan family and certainly no aristocrat, bursts out with the words: "He has brought down the mighty from their thrones and exalted those of humble estate; he has filled the hungry with good things, and the rich he has sent away empty" (Luke 1:52–53).
- Jesus consistently seeks out those who are, in one way or another, marginalized in the society of his day:
  - Those disadvantaged by family circumstance: widows and orphans.
  - Those looked down upon because of their occupation or social choices: "sinners," prostitutes, and tax collectors.

- Those marginalized because of a physical disability: the blind and the lame.
- Those marginalized because of their age: children.
- Those marginalized because of their gender: women.
- Those marginalized because of their religion: the "good" Samaritan.

- Jesus's disciples are drawn mainly from the laboring class who, although they are not the destitute poor, are far from the sort of acolytes that a typical first-century Jewish rabbi would want to be seen gathering to himself.
- Jesus's preaching about the kingdom of God consistently emphasizes a reversal in fortunes: "Blessed are you who are hungry now, for you shall be satisfied. Blessed are you who weep now, for you shall laugh" (Luke 6:21), summed up as: "The last will be first, and the first last" (Matt. 20:16).
- In his letters, most fully in 1 and 2 Corinthians, Paul echoes the same theme when he writes, to mention but three among many examples, of God's foolish wisdom and weak strength (1 Cor. 1), of keeping treasure in jars of clay (2 Cor. 4:7), and of a "light momentary affliction" which "is preparing for us an eternal weight of glory beyond all comparison" (2 Cor. 4:17).

The theme's biblical center of gravity, however, is the incarnation, death, and resurrection of Jesus Christ: the eternal and majestic God becomes a frail human being to die the most shameful of deaths, an act which—paradoxically—is his greatest victory and eternal glory. This is the ultimate referent for each instance of the "great reversal" move, and it is on these central events that the analysis below will focus.

This dynamic of the great reversal, as we shall see, opens out onto a rhythm of life, an ethic, and a way of looking at and living in the world. Limiting our discussion to this salient biblical idea will both make an engagement with Foucault's thought feasible in the space available and also provide a coherence to the various thoughts and responses to Foucault's work offered below, allowing us to address the themes of history, power, and identity without having to lay a new biblical framework each time.

5

CRUCIFORM HISTORY:
PHILIPPIANS 2:5–11

Foucault's notion of history, it will be remembered, rejects a Hegelian totalizing approach and takes on board much of Nietzsche's disjunctive account. But how does the Bible understand the course of history? Is it an unbroken, totalizing dialectic or a series of dislocations, interruptions, or ruptures? The answer is: neither. The picture of history given in the Bible is neither straightforwardly progressive (even in a dialectical mode) nor irremediably disjunctive. Rather, it sits athwart that opposition, diagonalizing it.[1] One of the passages in which this emerges most clearly is Philippians 2:5–11, considered by many commentators to be an early hymnic or liturgical fragment incorporated into Paul's letter:

---

1. I elaborate the notion of biblical diagonalization at some length both in my book on Derrida in P&R's Great Thinkers series, and in *Thinking through Creation* (Phillipsburg, NJ: P&R Publishing, 2017). It is a term to describe the way in which a biblical position very frequently cuts across the options conceivable from a nonbiblical point of view, refusing a false dichotomy in order to sit athwart its neat categories and combine elements from each of them in surprising ways.

Have this mind among yourselves, which is yours in Christ Jesus, who, though he was in the form of God, did not count equality with God a thing to be grasped, but emptied himself, by taking the form of a servant, being born in the likeness of men. And being found in human form, he humbled himself by becoming obedient to the point of death, even death on a cross. Therefore God has highly exalted him and bestowed on him the name that is above every name, so that at the name of Jesus every knee should bow, in heaven and on earth and under the earth, and every tongue confess that Jesus Christ is Lord, to the glory of God the Father. (Phil. 2:5–11)

In this chapter, I will draw out of this passage and other sources a biblical view of history that charts a course through continuity and disjunction that is different from that followed by either Hegel or Foucault, a course that also begins to present a countermove to Foucault's account of Christianity as a religion of renunciation.

Dialectic, Rupture, and the Great Reversal

The first thing we can notice from Philippians 2 is that the direction of Christ's movement is not linear, in the sense that it does not continue in the same direction throughout. The passage consists first of a movement of descent from "equality with God" through the incarnation to death on the cross (vv. 5–8), followed by a movement of ascent from death to a place of high exaltation and a name above every other name (vv. 9–11). Note also that the pronouns in the passage indicate a rupture of agency at the point of the cross: it is Christ who humbles himself, but God who exalts him.

We can characterize this double movement as a "v-shaped" dynamic, with the downward stroke of the v representing Christ's self-humbling to death on a cross, and the upward stroke representing God's exaltation of Christ to the highest place. The cross, situated at the nadir of the two movements, is (literally as well as figuratively) the crucial moment in this dynamic.

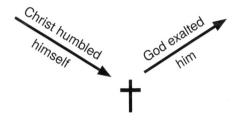

Fig. 5.1. The V-Shaped Dynamic of Philippians 2.

It would be reductive, however, to see this v-shaped movement as a mere reversal in fortunes (Christ is powerful, becomes weak, and then become powerful again), and at this point the biblical dynamic shares Foucault's rejection of Marx's account of revolution (even though Marx himself was drawing heavily on Christian eschatology). Marx understands the inevitable revolutionary overthrow of the capitalist land-owning class in terms of one group (the proletariat) wresting power from the hands of another group (the bourgeoisie). This means a transition from a hierarchy of power that can be represented like this:

BOURGEOISIE
_____
proletariat

Fig. 5.2. The bourgeoisie oppress the proletariat.

to one that can be represented like this:

PROLETARIAT
_____
bourgeoisie

Fig. 5.3. The roles of the bourgeoisie and the proletariat are reversed, but the structure remains unchanged.

In other words, the Marxist theory of revolution requires, at least in the period directly following the revolution, a reversal of fortunes, with a position of power previously occupied by the bourgeoisie now being filled by the proletariat. It is, in this sense, a straight swap, with the expectation that over time a classless society will develop in which terms like "proletariat" and "bourgeoisie" will no longer have any meaning.

If only the oppressed could seize power themselves, the idea goes, then they would wield it for the good of all and the problem of oppression would be solved. No doubt there is some truth to this, but, as Foucault foresees, it is a truth much more limited than orthodox Marxism would care to admit. For Foucault, the problem with this model of Marxist revolution is that it is too simple, reducing the different relations of power in society to one dominant factor: social class. Like Foucault, Philippians 2 also presents a more complex picture of the relation between the lord and the servant, between power and weakness, but it is also significantly different from Foucault's own account of capillary power.

Christ's Death on the Cross Resists a Linear Account of the Path to Glory

The specificity of this more complex picture hangs on the place of the cross in relation to Christ's glory. Some have tried to read Christ's crucifixion as a mere bump in the road on the way to exaltation, rather than a truly disjunctive moment. The argument goes like this: Knowing that he would eventually be glorified, Christ's death cannot be considered a "real" death, but only a strategic move that was necessary on his way to gaining power. "As I suspected," the skeptic might think, "the humility of the cross was just a temporary staging post for the Christ who always knew he would spend eternity being worshipped. A few hours of pain and three days of death for an eternity of adulation:

who would not shake on that deal?" This might have been a true appraisal of the case, had the exalted Jesus turned out to be a tyrant after all, with his humility a far-distant memory. But the Bible's account is very different from this reading of Christ's humility as a mere staging post, for two main reasons.

The first reason is the crucially important change of pronoun between verses 8 and 9: Christ made himself nothing, humbled himself, became obedient, and died on the cross, but did not exalt himself and did not give himself the name above every name. Christ humbled himself, but it is God who exalted him: there is a very clear disjunction in agency in this nonlinear account. This is not a ruse on Christ's part to wrest power for himself; there is a moment of dislocation between his self-humbling and his exaltation by another. This change of pronoun also challenges—just as Foucault does—the "great men" paradigm of history, according to which the outstanding genius, politician, or general is the primary driver of historical change. Christ cannot occupy, in the story of Philippians 2, this traditional position of greatness because he is passive in his own ascent to power. His only action in the passage is to humble and empty himself. He is glorified, not because he wins a war, rules a nation, makes a fortune, writes a great book, or inspires a crowd. He is not strictly glorified because he empties himself and dies, as if it were a quid pro quo. Christ is obedient to his Father, and it pleases the Father to exalt him. Foucault and the Bible, in their different ways, both subvert the narrative according to which history is the story of the great deeds of self-made "great men."

There is a second reason why it is incorrect to read Christ's humiliation as a ruse cloaking a linear and uninterrupted path to power: rather than serving as a temporary way station on Christ's inevitable ascent to glory, the cross is taken in the biblical account to be a moment that defines his identity into eternity. In Revelation 5, for instance, John repeatedly refers to the figure of a (sacrificial) lamb on the throne of heaven, a lamb "standing, as though it had been slain" (Rev. 5:6). The cross is not quickly forgotten as the resurrected Christ dusts himself off and resumes a position of power. It is not a necessary-but-transient moment of grubbiness on his ascent up the greasy pole to glory. It is his glory (see Rev. 5:12, 13; 7:9–10, 13; 21:23).

J. Joyce Schuld brings out well the contrast between this non-linear heavenly glory and linear paths to earthly power:

> This glorification, in contrast to earthly glorification, does not eliminate humility and lowliness but raises them to new purposes. The "shame of the cross" is not left behind or negated. It is "re-formed," along with the sinful, so as to structure their service back to the world.[2]

The fulfillment of Philippians 2:9–10 will be the worship, not of the self-glorified king, but of the God-glorified Lamb. The one who is worshipped in glory in Philippians 2:9–10 is the humbled Jesus, the Jesus of the cross, the one whom John the Baptist proclaimed as the "lamb of God" (John 1:36), and the Jesus of Philippians 2:6–8. Every knee will bow and every tongue confess the crucified-glorified Jesus as Lord. Let it be clearly understood, at this point, that the Christ of Philippians 2 is not a Christ who is all weakness and no power, as if the chapter finished at the end of verse 8. This is what some have tried to argue, and it presents a distorted picture of how the Bible presents Christ's relation to power. The picture that emerges from Philippians 2 is not of a weak or powerless Christ, but of a Christ whose power is of a particular, nonlinear kind that subverts the narrative according to which power is something that must be won or grabbed.

---

2. J. Joyce Schuld, *Foucault and Augustine: Reconsidering Power and Love* (Notre Dame, IN: Notre Dame University Press, 2003), 121.

Why is the picture of power that emerges in Philippians 2 significant for our purposes in this volume? Because in his death and resurrection, Christ subverts the perennial dichotomy between the lord and the servant, between the humbled and the glorified: the Lord is forever the Servant, and the Servant is forever the Lord. This is a more profound attack on the lord-servant dichotomy than any proletarian revolution or anarchist commune, because it subverts the structures of oppression and exploitation sustained by that dichotomy, rather than merely changing who it is that occupies the places marked out within those structures. Christ sets a new pattern for the exercise of authority and power: the master, the one in authority, is the one who looks, not to his own needs, but to the needs of others, and, as Paul stresses in verse 5, Jesus's followers are to imitate him in this. Abusive authority is subverted from the inside by attacking its binary structure, rather than from the outside by changing the labels on the positions within the binary structure. The master is not overthrown; the master becomes (and remains) a servant. This does not only reverse the prevailing relations of power; it challenges the very structure of those relations, cutting across or "diagonalizing" the otherwise binary categories:

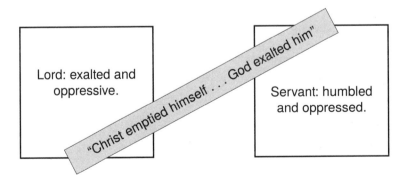

Fig. 5.4. Philippians 2 diagonalizes the dichotomy of oppressive, exalted power and oppressed, humble servanthood.

Unlike Foucault's account of disciplinary power cutting off the head of the king and yet installing a regime of control even deeper and more insidious than that of sovereign power, this diagonalization leaves the king's head on his shoulders, but gives him—so to speak—a brain transplant, subverting the logic of oppressor/oppressed and inaugurating a new paradigm of society in which power is no longer understood in the old, linear way of the strong lording it over the weak. It does not simply mark a temporary hiatus in the historical paradigm according to which strength prevails over weakness and the powerful inevitably rise to the top; nor does it merely reverse the labels attached to the generic categories "oppressive" and "oppressed." By breaking with the very logic of linear power, the great reversal marks a radical disjunction that can be never be brought back into the old linear logic.

The way in which the reversal motif functions bears striking similarities to Foucault's stated aim for his own writing: to show that things can be otherwise. Glossing the moment in Genesis 25 in which God chooses the younger son Jacob over his elder brother Esau,[3] Walter Brueggemann comments:

> This oracle speaks about an inversion. It affirms that we are not fated to the way the world is presently organized. That is the premise of the ministry of Jesus: the poor, the mourning, the meek, the hungry . . . are the heirs to the kingdom. (Matt. 5:3–7)[4]

This is the same premise that Foucault wishes for his own writing when he describes the "'effective' history" that "deprives the self

3. "And the LORD said to her, 'Two nations are in your womb, and two peoples from within you shall be divided; the one shall be stronger than the other, the older shall serve the younger'" (Gen. 25:23).

4. Walter Brueggemann, *Genesis* (Atlanta: John Knox, 1982), 215.

of the reassuring stability of life and nature" and which "will not permit itself to be transported by a voiceless obstinacy toward a millennial ending" (*EW2-AME*, 380). Both Foucault's histories and the biblical motif of reversal prevent us from becoming comfortable in the thought that things will always be as they currently are.

Christ's Death on the Cross Resists Hegelian Sublation

If Christ's death cannot be construed as a temporary, cynical gesture that can be neatly incorporated into the story of a linear ascent to power, then neither does the biblical account fit snugly into Hegel's dialectical reading of the incarnation, death, and resurrection of Christ. It is worth taking a little time to distinguish the Bible's nonlinear or v-shaped idea of history from Hegel's dialectic, not least because Hegel himself thought that the incarnation, death, and resurrection fitted his own model rather well.

Christianity, for Hegel, is a story about the abstract and the concrete, the infinite and the finite. He divides biblical history into three ages: the age of the Father, of the Son, and of the Spirit.

- The Father, who is eternal Idea, creates a concrete universe and a finite humanity. This opposition between infinite God and finite creation is the opposition that Hegel's account of Christianity seeks to overcome.
- God must become man in Jesus Christ, uniting the infinite (God) and the finite (human beings). The incarnate Christ is a concrete universal, both absolute and embodied.
- Christ's death on the cross is understood as a self-negation of God, a moment that breaks the exclusive union between Christ and the Father in a way that prepares for Hegel's account of the resurrection.

- Resurrection itself is understood, not as Christ's bodily rising, but as an event in the Christian community, a "spiritual resurrection"[5] of "universal self-consciousness"[6] (i.e., the religious community now knows itself as the embodiment of the Idea). The whole community now shares in the union with God previously enjoyed only by Christ.
- Pentecost ushers in the new age of the Spirit, succeeding the ages of the Father and the Son. In this third age, the opposition between humanity and God is "sublated" or overcome because they are now united in Absolute Spirit.
- In short, the incarnation, death, and resurrection of Christ for Hegel are most important as metaphors for the coming to self-awareness of the Christian community.

This process brings about not only a change in humanity (it is now conscious of itself as an expression of God-the-Idea), but also a change in God himself, as Hegel explains:

> God, as an abstraction, is not true God, but only as the living process of positing his Other, the world, which comprehended in its divine form is His Son; and it is only in unity with his other, in Spirit, that God is Subject.[7]

God realizes himself through humanity, incorporating into himself the finitude and concreteness that he previously lacked. God becomes "true God," as Hegel says, in the death and resurrection of Christ and in the outpouring of the Spirit at Pentecost. This story, as many commentators point out, is much more concerned

---

5. G. W. F. Hegel, *The Phenomenology of Mind*, trans. J. B. Baillie (London: Routledge, 2015), §784, 2:793.

6. Ibid., §785, 2:794–95.

7. G. W. F. Hegel, *Hegel's Philosophy of Nature*, trans. A. V. Miller (Oxford: Oxford University Press, 2004), §246, 13.

to be faithful to Hegel's own system of speculative philosophy than it is to the biblical account.

There are fundamental differences between the Hegelian system and the biblical material. First of all, it is hard to press the biblical account into three distinct stages governed by the Father, the Son, and the Spirit, respectively. The Spirit is present at creation (Gen. 1:2) and so is Christ (Col. 1:16), for example. Neither the Father nor the Son retreats from the scene in the final book of the Bible. Second, there is no hint in the biblical accounts that God comes to self-realization through the incarnation, death, and resurrection of Christ, or through the pouring out of the Spirit at Pentecost. God is complete in his Trinitarian existence before creation, and complete after creation without needing anything from his creatures, as Paul explains to the assembled philosophers of Athens:

> The God who made the world and everything in it, being Lord of heaven and earth, does not live in temples made by man, nor is he served by human hands, as though he needed anything, since he himself gives to all mankind life and breath and everything. (Act 17:24–25)

Furthermore, the notion that finitude is the gulf to be overcome between God and humanity owes more to some currents of ancient Greek philosophy and to the dictates of Hegel's speculative system than it does to the Bible. For the Bible, the human problem is not finitude but God's wrath against sin, and Christ in his death does not embrace finitude, but bears sin (1 Peter 2:24). If Hegel were correct that the great triumph of Christ was to incorporate finitude into the infinite, then we might expect a man on the throne of heaven in Revelation 5, but instead we see a lamb. The focus of the biblical narrative is not on the finite/infinite distinction, but on "the Lamb of God, who takes away the sin of the world" (John 1:29). In those biblical passages where it is stated that, through Christ, all things will be united in God (Eph. 1:10), there is no suggestion that God requires this reconciliation in order to be truly God or to realize himself. In short, the biblical narrative of creation, incarnation, death, resurrection, and Pentecost loses its identity if it is conformed to a speculative system in which God is in need of self-realization.

Rupture of What?

As we have seen, Foucault's history of rupture and disjunction "deprives the self of the reassuring stability of life and nature" (*EW2-AME*, 380) and has the effect of showing people that "they are much freer than they feel" (TPS, 10). We have also seen that a similar consequence can be drawn from the biblical great reversal. Nevertheless, there are significant differences between rupture in Foucault's historiography and disjunction in the biblical account. For example, Foucault's ruptures are local (restricted as they are to Western and even French culture), whereas the biblical great reversal is universal. The rupture of the great reversal is also, in an important sense, more fundamental than Foucault's epistemic ruptures, as I shall now try to show.

The most significant difference between the two accounts of rupture can be discerned if we ask, "What is ruptured or dislocated?" For Foucault, the rupture is epistemic: it is the way in which we understand the world, the categories we use to make sense of it, and the way that power is distributed and circulates within society. There is, however, underlying these historical ruptures, an important continuity in the assumptions that undergird Foucault's account of the different modes of power relations. For example, sovereign power and disciplinary power are both modes of what Foucault calls "action upon the action of others" (EW3-P, 345–46). Whether it occurs in the mode of sovereign power or the mode of disciplinary power, the assumptions necessary for power to be "action upon the action of others" (including the division between self and other, the ascription of action to an actor, and so forth) remain constant. Where there is no rupture, for Foucault, is in these underlying assumptions that run through the different modes of power relations.

For Foucault, then, history may well be amenable to analysis in terms of successive epistemes, but each of these epistemes is a new move in the same game of power relations: there is no qualitative break in the regime of power, no nonlinear rupture or interruption of power per se by something outside or beyond it. Sovereign power, pastoral power, disciplinary power, and biopower all operate in the same way, acting upon the action of others according to a variety of modalities. Foucault, in other words, thinks in terms of breaks between forms of power, but he does not (nor does he want or think it possible) to fracture the underlying assumptions that run across these accounts, whether we summarize those assumptions with the shorthand "action upon the action of others" or in another way. In this sense, for Foucault, the account of power across historical periods is linear, despite his insistence on Nietzschean epistemic ruptures.

The biblical rupture of the great reversal, by contrast, is nonlinear. The movement from incarnation to cross to resurrection does not merely break with a particular historical mode of power relations (shifting the dominant paradigm from sovereign to disciplinary power, for example); rather, it fractures the very oppositions (between master and servant, will and renunciation, sovereignty and obedience) that all these accounts of power assume at one level or another. In the work of Foucault and Nietzsche, we see ruptures within the history of power, but in the great reversal we see a rupture in the prerequisites and structure of power relations themselves.

Similarly, if we think about it in terms of time, the great reversal does not simply mark a rupture between successive epistemes within time, but confronts time itself with its other, with eternity, with the Christ who was "in the beginning" (Gen. 1:1; John 1:1) with God "before" (so to speak) the creation of chronological time, and the lamb who was "foreknown before the foundation of the world" (1 Peter 1:20). Foucault's epistemic shifts create ruptures only *within* time, in the sense that each episteme exists in what Charles Taylor in *A Secular Age* calls "secular time" or "profane time": the everyday time of successive days, months, years, and millennia.[8] The biblical great reversal, by contrast, ruptures secular time itself by opening it to the "higher time" of an eternity which it cannot incorporate as merely an infinite extension of secular moments (for the Christian notion of eternity, as Taylor helpfully points out, is understood, following Augustine, not as an infinite succession of moments, nor as an atemporal immobility, but as a gathering together of all time into an instant).[9]

So to conclude this rather dense section, Foucault and the Bible are agreed in seeing temporal rupture as a way to show that things can be different from how they currently are, but the Bible's rupture is more fundamental than Foucault's and shows that more can be different. Whereas Foucault's ruptures occur within secular, linear time, the great reversal ruptures linear time itself.

Christ's Gesture Is Not One of Self-Renunciation, but Self-Giving

One further issue that can be addressed from the Philippians 2 passage is Foucault's characterization of Christianity as a religion of renunciation. Christ's actions in the passage might seem to be a prime example of self-renunciation: Christ empties himself, taking the form of a servant, humbling himself, being obedient

8. Charles Taylor, *A Secular Age* (Cambridge, MA: Harvard University Press, 2006), 55–61.

9. Ibid., 57.

even to death. It cuts against the grain of biblical language, however, to say that Christ renounces himself and his own will in being obedient to death; the language used in the Bible is that he gives himself (Gal. 1:4; 2:20; Eph. 5:2, 25; Titus 2:6; 2:14). The Bible's preferred language of self-giving is not a negative gesture of self-denial, but a positive initiative for the sake of the other. Sarah Coakley treads this biblical path well when she argues that

> the "vulnerability" that is its human condition is not about asking for unnecessary and unjust suffering (though increased self-knowledge can be indeed be painful); nor is it a "self-abnegation." On the contrary, the special "self-emptying" is not a negation of self, but the place of the self's transformation and expansion into God.[10]

There is more to Christ's self-humbling than self-renunciation, and therefore more to Christian self-humbling than self-renunciation as well. There is an irreducible outward-facing direction to Christ's humbling and exultation, and therefore also to the pattern of Christian life and behavior, which prevents it from becoming an insular path either of self-renunciation or of its mirror image, self-aggrandizement. The focus, furthermore, is not generically outward, but precisely Godward, as Augustine well captures in *The City of God*:

> The earthly city glories in itself, the Heavenly City glories in the Lord. The former looks for glory from men, the latter finds its highest glory in God, the witness of a good conscience. The earthly lifts up its head in its own glory, the Heavenly City says to its God: "My Glory; you lift up my head." . . . The one city

10. Sarah Coakley, *Powers and Submissions: Spirituality, Philosophy and Gender* (Oxford: Blackwell, 2008), 36.

loves its own strength shown in its powerful leaders; the other says to its God, "I will love you, my Lord, my strength."[11]

Christ's descent in Philippians 2:6–8 is a radical openness to the other in the sense that it is a complete self-emptying (to the point of the cross) in order to be filled by the other.

The Asymmetry of Obedience to God

One thing that Foucault does not take into account—or rather, is unable to think, given his atheism—is a relationship of self-giving to the other that is not a straightforwardly heteronomous renunciation of self. Indeed, if what is at stake is the renunciation of the will to another human agent, then this would indeed be such a heteronomous act. What Foucault's bracketing of theology in favor of church institutions forbids him from considering, however, is that the Christian's relationship with God cannot be patterned on the relationship between two human beings, and that to obey God is not the same thing as to obey anyone else.

The relationship between any two human beings is, in principle, symmetrical; neither has an ontological right to exert an absolute command over the other.

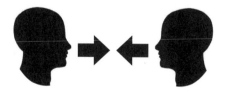

Fig. 5.5. Symmetry: the ontological equality between any two people means that neither has the inherent right to command the other.

11. Augustine, *The City of God* (Harmondsworth: Penguin, 2004), 14.28, p. 593.

The relationship between Creator and creature, however, is asymmetrical in significant ways: God created human beings, who are his workmanship (Act 17:24–26); we are utterly contingent for our very existence upon his ongoing work of upholding us (Heb. 1:3; Col. 1:17); we were created both in his image and for him (Col. 1:16). So to renounce my will to God is a qualitatively different act than renouncing it to a fellow human being, for I am renouncing it not to one who is completely other to me, but to the one who is, to quote Augustine's famous passage from his *Confessions*, "interior intimo meo et superior summo meo" (higher than my highest and more inward than my innermost self) (*Confessions*, III, 6, 11).

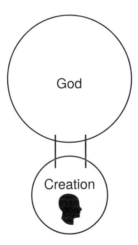

Fig. 5.6. Asymmetry: God is not my ontological equal. His command upholds my being moment by moment.

The God-human relationship cannot be assimilated to a human-human relationship for the additional reason that I, as a Christian, am "in Christ," united to him in a way that is deeper than any intimacy between two autonomous and independent human beings.

As we have seen, Foucault defines power, in an interview entitled "The Subject and Power" (first published in 1982), as "action upon the action of others" (*EW3-P*, 342–46). The formulation presupposes both a distinction and an ontological symmetry between the two actors. In the case of God, however, it is incorrect to say that he acts upon my action, for that formula assumes that I can be considered autonomous from the action of God in the first place, such that his action can supervene upon a situation from which it was previously absent. According to the biblical view, by contrast, God's action frames and sustains me moment by moment, making possible any action of my own, and this relationship in which my existence and action are contingent on God cannot be reduced to the reciprocity assumed by Foucault's definition.

Renunciation, Realization, Obedience

In the context of this radical asymmetry in the relationship between God and human beings, to renounce my will to God is not to condemn myself to a life devoid of pleasure and full of *ressentiment*; nor, on the other hand, is it a program of self-realization. Foucault seems to see nothing in Christianity but renunciation of pleasure and a miserable forfeiting of one's own will to the will of God and to his appointed authorities, engendering a *ressentiment* in the pleasure-deprived believer. John Milbank critiques this Foucauldian position by arguing that the goal of Christian renunciation is self-realization, not self-negation:

> Foucault is, of course, aware that desire necessarily implies a radical orientation to the other, but instead of interpreting this as a structuring of the self in terms of goal and aspiration, he takes it as implying a pure heterogeneity, a handing of the self over to the spiritual director or to God. What he ignores here is that total obedience, in the former case, assumes a prior agreement

that the director is further advanced towards the goal that the postulant wishes to arrive at, so that *self-realization (given this understanding of the self), not self-negation, is here presupposed.*[12]

I am not sure, however, that either Foucault or Milbank captures the cruciform dynamic of Philippians 2. Humility—which Paul offers as a model for the Philippian Christians' own attitude toward each other—is not a miserable drudge of self-negation, but it does it no justice to call it a journey of self-realization, either. The emphasis on self-renunciation reduces the v-shaped dynamic to its downward stroke, and the focus on self-realization thinks only of its upward stroke. Self-realization retains (along with self-renunciation) a certain linear dynamic: I plan to realize in the future a self that I project and desire in the present. But the zero point of utter self-emptying on the cross and the radical transformation of resurrected life make any such linear account of self-realization inimical to this cruciform dynamic. In chapter 7, we shall also see how desire itself is transformed at the cross, rupturing any model of straightforward self-realization.

There is more to say than the positions of both self-renunciation and self-realization will allow, because Christ's self-emptying is not simply a self-renunciation, and his exaltation is not simply a self-realization. It is the pattern followed by the Paul who can say:

> I count everything as loss because of the surpassing worth of knowing Christ Jesus my Lord. For his sake I have suffered the loss of all things and count them as rubbish, in order that I may gain Christ and be found in him. (Phil. 3:8–9)

---

12. John Milbank, *Theology and Social Theory: Beyond Secular Reason*, 2nd ed. (Oxford: Blackwell, 2006), 202 (emphasis added).

To read Foucault, we would think that Jesus had not said, "Whoever would save his life will lose it, but whoever loses his life for my sake will find it," but rather, "Whoever would save his life will lose it, and whoever loses it for my sake will also lose it" (from Matt. 16:25), and that Paul had not said "Christ . . . though he was rich, yet for your sake he became poor, so that you by his poverty might become rich," but rather, "Christ . . . though he was rich, yet for your sake he became poor, so that you by his poverty might become poor as well" (from 2 Cor. 8:9). Foucault's portrait of sullen Christian renunciation is a warning against sub-biblical legalism or blindly following religious teachers, but it ignores the dynamics of the biblical account of the Christian's self-giving to God.

So, to conclude this chapter, what account of history does this passage from Philippians 2 give us, in its biblical context? It offers a paradigm for understanding world history that resolves neither to Hegelian dialectic nor to a Nietzschean/Foucauldian disjunctive succession of epistemes. If Hegel offers us a dialectic, totalizing account of history, and Foucault/Nietzsche offer a disjunctive, dislocated account, then the Bible offers us a non-linear, v-shaped account of history, the pattern of which is the incarnation, death, and resurrection of Jesus Christ. This biblical account does not reject Foucault out of hand; in fact, it shares his mistrust of the linear, Enlightenment notion of history as an unbroken and inevitable progression with improvement building upon improvement toward a final perfection. Nor, however, does it affirm Foucault's own strategy of resisting this Enlightenment totalization through a history of ruptures. Whereas such ruptures are, as we have seen, within the basic structures of power relations, Philippians 2 begins to sketch for us a way of rupturing those structural prerequisites of power themselves. It is in further pursuit of this biblical disruption of the prerequisites of power in the great reversal that we now turn to 1 Corinthians 1.

6

CRUCIFORM POWER:
1 CORINTHIANS 1:18 – 31

In the previous chapter, we saw how the Bible offers an account of history that resolves neither to Hegelian dialectical progress nor to Foucauldian/Nietzschean disjunction, an understanding characterized by a v-shaped movement of self-emptying and exaltation by another that resists Hegel's dialectic and effects a rupture more fundamental than Foucault's. In the present chapter, we will elaborate further on the biblical motif of the great reversal in relation to the theme of power, expanding the v-shaped movement to become an x-shaped figure centering on the cross. The theme of the great reversal touches the motif of power explicitly in 1 Corinthians 1, and that chapter will furnish the core of our reflections. I will first show how Paul sets out a paradigm of cruciform power that, like Foucault's account, challenges the simple binary of sovereignty as a dyad of ruler and ruled, and then I will discuss how it offers an equally strong challenge to Foucault's own understanding of power.

God's Weak Power and Foolish Wisdom

"For Jews Demand Signs and Greeks Seek Wisdom" (v. 22)

In 1 Corinthians 1, Paul identifies two dominant values, one in the Greek view of the world and one in the Jewish.

- First, Jews demand signs (*semeion*, 1:22), that is, miraculous events. It is unclear from this brief phrase alone what it is that the Jews prize in such miracles, but Paul makes it clear as the passage progresses by substituting the wisdom/signs dyad of 1:22 with a wisdom/power distinction in 1:24. What the Jews desire is a direct demonstration of God's supernatural power in miraculous form.
- Second, Greeks seek wisdom (*sophia*), one of the root words of the English term "philosophy." From the surrounding context in 1 Corinthians, it appears that the aspect of wisdom that Paul particularly has in mind is rhetorical impressiveness and skill in debating. In verse 17, he tells the Corinthians that Christ sent him to preach "not with words of eloquent wisdom [*sophia*], lest the cross of Christ be emptied of its power," and in verse 20 he asks, "Where is the one who is wise? Where is the scribe? Where is the debater of this age? Has not God made foolish the wisdom [*sophia*] of the world?"

So both "signs" and "wisdom," as Paul presents them in this passage, are direct manifestations of power and prowess, cowing those who witness them into submission, either by a superior demonstration of rhetorical skill or by the raw power of an impressive miracle. For reasons that I hope will become increasingly clear as this chapter progresses, I propose to represent this demand for signs and wisdom as a line ascending from left to right, the rising trajectory indicating that signs and wisdom embody, for those who seek them, a positive gain and something to be desired.

Fig. 6.1. Paul identifies dominant values in Jewish and Greek culture.

"But We Preach Christ Crucified" (v. 23a)

Jews demand signs and Greeks seek wisdom, but what they get from Paul is the word (*logos*, 1:18) of the cross. No amount of highfalutin rhetoric on my part could hope to convey to a contemporary readership the outrageous nature of the words "Christ crucified" to ancient ears. A comment from Cicero's *Pro Rabiro* is often trotted out by writers who feel powerless—as I do here—to convey the scandal of the cross to modern readers: "The very word 'cross' should be far removed not only from the person of a Roman citizen but from his thoughts, his eyes and his ears."[1] The cross was considered such a shameful and degrading form of death, we are reminded, that no Roman citizen could be subjected to it. So to claim for the cross anything like "wisdom" or "power" must have struck Corinthian ears as sarcastic and absurd. As Kathy Ehrensperger explains:

> To seek support for authority claims via an emphasis on weakness and suffering could be seen as anachronistic in the

---

1. Cicero, "In Defense of Rabirius," in *The Speeches of Cicero*, trans. H. G. Lodge (London: Heinemann, 1927), 467.

Hellenistic and Roman world where such experiences gave rise to contempt and intimidation rather than recognition and respect. . . . To relate authority claims to weakness and suffering seems at least paradoxical if not foolish from the perspective of a society which was saturated with values of strength and competitive dominating power.[2]

The method of crucifixion itself, in fact, is a demonstration of just such dominating power, a political statement (as in the climax of the Spartacus story, made famous by the 1960 Kirk Douglas movie) warning of extreme consequences for anyone who would seek to challenge Roman sovereign power. The "Christ" (Greek *christos*, equivalent to the Hebrew *mâshîyach*, root of the English *messiah*, both of which mean "anointed") was understood as the one who would lead his people to victory according to the pattern of military conquest laid down by King David, "the anointed [*mâshîyach*] of the God of Jacob" (2 Sam. 23:1). The story of King David, who "killed his tens of thousands," is very far indeed from the shame of the cross. So the phrase "the power of the cross" would most readily have been understood by first-century minds as referring to a show of Roman might, and certainly not as suggesting that the crucified one demonstrates power in any sense. Searching for modern equivalents, "the vagrant king" or "the executed emperor" do not come close to the oxymoronic scandal of the crucified Messiah.

On our developing diagram, "Christ crucified" is represented on a line descending from left to right, reprising the downward trajectory of Christ's self-emptying from Philippians 2.

---

2. Kathy Ehrensperger, *Paul and the Dynamics of Power: Communication and Interaction in the Early Christ-Movement* (London: T&T Clark, 1997), 98.

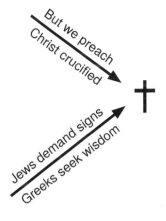

Fig. 6.2. Paul's Message of Christ Crucified.

"A Stumbling Block to Jews and Folly to Gentiles" (v. 23b)

This message of Christ crucified, Paul goes on to note, is seen by Jews and Gentiles alike as singularly unable to satiate their cultural thirst for wisdom and power. For the Greeks who seek wisdom, the cross is stupid (*moria,* from which we get "moronic"), and for the Jews, searching for a miraculous manifestation of God's power, it is a "stumbling block" (*skandalon,* which can be translated both as "offense" and "means of stumbling," and is the root of the modern English "scandal"). The combined judgment of Jews and Greeks is that the cross is stupid and offensive.

Given that we anticipate where Paul is going with this argument—especially if we are Christians in sympathy with Paul's argument—the reasoning of the Jews and Greeks can be dismissed too easily at this point. It is worth stressing, then, that the Jews and Greeks have a strong commonsense case, as Paul Helm is at pains to emphasize in *The Providence of God*:

> In physical combat, the unarmed man is likely to lose; the person who repudiates the role of a revolutionary or political

leader is unlikely to gain a following from the dissatisfied or from those with ambitions for success. In the normal means-end thinking that governs the activities of rational and intelligent people, political success comes from political effort, and it is foolish to hope for success from a cross.[3]

The Jews and Greeks who dismiss the cross as offensive stupidity are doing nothing more or less than obeying what Carl Trueman calls "the canons of meaning operative in the world around [them]."[4] It is the reasonable conclusion of linear thinking: strength wins; wisdom wins.

This dismissal of the cross on the grounds of its offensive stupidity is represented in our diagram by a descending line leading downward to the right of the cross: Jews and Greeks have failed to find the power and wisdom they were looking for in the cross and are repulsed by it, turning away from it.

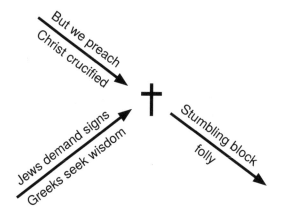

Fig. 6.3. The canons of the age dismiss the message of the cross.

3. Paul Helm, *The Providence of God* (Leicester: Inter-Varsity Press, 1994), 226.
4. Carl R. Trueman, *Luther on the Christian Life: Cross and Freedom* (Wheaton, IL: Crossway Books, 2015), 64.

The experience of the Jews and Greeks in Paul's discourse can therefore be traced as the caret shape (^) forming the lower half of the diagram: seeking powerful signs and wisdom, they encounter Paul's word of the cross and find in it only folly and a stumbling block.

"But to Those Who Are Called, Both Jews and Greeks, Christ the Power of God and the Wisdom of God" (v. 24)

The fourth and final observation which will help us to draw an understanding of power out of 1 Corinthians 1 is that the crucified Christ is the power and wisdom of God. This is a twist in the argument that was just as likely to raise ancient hackles and smirks as the affirmation that God's Messiah could be crucified. According to Paul, it is at the cross, seemingly the least likely of all places, that the cultural aspirations of the Jews (for power) and the Greeks (for wisdom) find their ultimate fulfillment.

Once more, Paul Helm helps us to see what Paul means—and, importantly, what he does not mean—when he refers to the power and wisdom of the cross:

> According to Paul, such wisdom and power is literally wisdom and power. It is not that the wisdom of the Greeks is literally wisdom, and the wisdom of the cross loosely or metaphorically or symbolically so. There is a moral or spiritual refraction which prevents all men and women seeing divine wisdom as such, but such it is. This is how God really is; God's moral and spiritual character is such that the cross is entirely congruous with it, and is perhaps (though this is more controversial) the only expression that divine wisdom and power could have taken when faced with the human predicament.[5]

5. Helm, *The Providence of God*, 226.

This is nonlinear thinking at its most aggressive. Recognizing the wisdom and power of the cross requires of us a complete transformation of what we understand wisdom and power to be. The passage is not challenging the Greeks and Jews to make do with some quirky divine imitation of the power and wisdom they are searching for; it is affirming that God's power is the only ultimate power and that God's wisdom is the only true wisdom, requiring the Greeks and Jews to transform their most cherished cultural values of wisdom and power in order to take account of this central reality. We can tag this necessary destruction of the old concepts of wisdom and power and their replacement with God's wisdom and power with the statement "Nothing passes through the cross untransformed." In other words, the Jewish cultural expectation of God's power will either be repulsed by the cross or, if it embraces it, that cultural value will be emptied out and rebuilt in the process, transfigured as it passes through the cross. Similarly, the Greek premium on rhetorical wisdom will either laugh at the cross as ridiculous and stupid (and as a result never find the ultimate fulfillment of what it is looking for) or, if it is willing to embrace the wisdom of the cross, will transform its previous understanding of wisdom in the process. The cross, once more, is a point of nonlinear disjunction and rupture. Wisdom and power are to be found there, but only if seekers are willing to countenance that they do not yet truly understand what they are seeking. Here we have a requirement for humility that ruptures the linear quest for power.

Let us note in passing that Paul is not dismissing the values of these two very different cultures out of hand. He is not saying that the search for wisdom is a misguided search, nor that the desire for power can never be fulfilled. He is not dismissing Jewish and Greek culture altogether. What he is saying is that these cultural values will never be found in any ultimate sense in those places where the Jews and the Greeks are presently looking for them. True wisdom and true power will be encountered only on condition of seeking them at the place that seems to be the epitome of their negation: the stupidity and offence of the cross. We can represent this in a line ascending to the right of the cross, now completing our diagram.

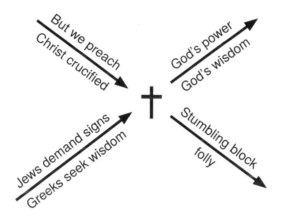

Fig. 6.4. The "Foolish" Wisdom and "Weak" Power of the Cross.

Now we can follow the whole bottom-left to top-right diagonal: if the search for power and wisdom is to find its object, then it must pass through the cross to find God's power and God's wisdom, for, as Paul reminds his readers, "the foolishness of God is wiser than men, and the weakness of God is stronger than men" (1 Cor. 1:25). We can also find again the v-shaped dynamic that we encountered in the Philippians 2 passage: Christ crucified is revealed as God's power and wisdom.

The difference between the v-trajectory and the ^-trajectory across this diagram is neatly captured in Martin Luther's distinction in the Heidelberg Disputation of 1518 between what he calls "theologians of glory" and "theologians of the cross." The theologian of glory, Luther argues, "looks upon the invisible things of God as though they were clearly perceptible in those things which have actually happened."[6] In other words, he looks for a linear continuity between, on the one hand, commonsense notions of power and wisdom, and, on the other hand, God's power and wisdom. He follows the ^-trajectory. As historian Carl Trueman explains, "the theologian of glory will no doubt understand the word *power*, when applied to God, as referring to something analogous to a king's power: imposing and coercive."[7]

In the very next thesis of the Heidelberg Disputation, Luther describes the theologian of the cross as one "who comprehends the visible and manifest things of God seen through suffering and the cross."[8] For the theologian of the cross, God's power is not merely greater than earthly power, but of a different quality. To a world that only knows one type of power—the type that turns all too easily into exploitation and oppression—the cross brings a message of raw power set aside in order to serve, of unchallengeable authority bracketed for the sake of serving others. Like Charles Taylor's account of the opening of secular time to eternity discussed in the previous chapter, the Bible here introduces a qualitative rupture in our understanding of power and wisdom.

Lest the power and wisdom of the cross be misunderstood, the claim here is not that weakness is itself powerful, nor that any manifestation of weakness is powerful, nor again that weakness is to be glorified for its own sake. Paul is not offering an apology for weakness and foolishness in themselves, but for the weakness and foolishness of the cross. He reports that when he pleaded for his thorn in the flesh to be taken away, he received the message from God, not that power in general is to be found

---

6. Timothy F. Lull and William R. Russell, eds., *Martin Luther's Basic Theological Writings* (Minneapolis: Fortress Press, 2012), 15.

7. Trueman, *Luther on the Christian Life*, 64.

8. Lull and Russell, eds., *Martin Luther's Basic Theological Writings*, 15.

in weakness, but that *"my* power is made perfect in weakness"
(2 Cor. 12:9). Similarly, it is going too far to sum up the dynamic
of the great reversal by saying, "The kingdom of God obeys the
law of reversals in virtue of which *whatever is* first is last, *whatever
is* out is in, *whatever* is lost is saved."[9] Such a law of reversal can
seek to control and manipulate God just as much as its mirror
image, according to which God is thought to privilege the rich
and powerful. Paul admonishes the Corinthians, not with the
words "not any," but with "not many of you were wise according
to worldly standards, not many were powerful, not many were of
noble birth" (1 Cor. 1:26).

Truth, Power, and Subversion

This cruciform transformation of power and wisdom provides a way to address one of the issues that causes a problem
for Foucault: the relation of his account of truth to his political
commitments. Foucault has two complaints against the notion of
transhistorical and transcultural truth: he thinks it is false, and he
thinks it is dangerous. It is false because, as he tries to show in his
archaeological and genealogical studies, concepts like madness
and sexuality do not remain stable over time, and to assume that
they do is just plain wrong: there are no "anthropological universals." The idea is dangerous because the notion of unchanging and binding truth forecloses the possibility of self-creation
and self-transformation that, for Foucault, is the motivation for
engaging in historical writing in the first place.

Foucault's own position is not that there is no truth. Indeed,
in a 1984 interview entitled "The Concern for Truth," he laments
that "all those who say that, for me, truth doesn't exist are being

---

9. John D. Caputo, *The Weakness of God: A Theology of the Event* (Bloomington,
IN: Indiana University Press, 2006), 14, emphasis added.

simplistic" (*PPC*, 257), and in place of this simplistic misunderstanding he offers the explanation that "what I am trying to do is to write the history of the relations between thought and truth; the history of thought as such is thought about truth" (*PPC*, 257). This is echoed in what has become Foucault's most famous pronouncement on the subject: "Truth is a thing of this world: it is produced only by virtue of multiple forms of constraint" (*P/K*, 131). A little further on in the same interview, he explains in more detail what it means for truth to be a thing of this world:

> Each society has its "general politics" of truth: that is, the types of discourse which it accepts and makes function as true; the mechanisms and instances which enable one to distinguish true and false statements, the means by which each is sanctioned; the techniques and procedures accorded value in the acquisition of truth; the status of those who are charged with saying what counts as true. (*P/K*, 131)

This quotation helps us to appreciate that truth, for Foucault, is a complex product of many forces and power relations within society, a product of the sorts of discourses which are accepted in the public square, a product of the legal, social, and personal processes which allow some statements to circulate and suppress others, of the privileged and permitted means of attaining what a given society labels "truth" (perhaps scientific, perhaps academic, perhaps mystical, perhaps through trial by ordeal in medieval Europe), and of the figures who carry the authority to speak this truth in public.

So for Foucault truth is contingent, complex, and limited (both temporally and geographically); it is something that is produced. As we have seen, however, Foucault must necessarily pay a twofold price for situating truth as "a thing of this world": a blindness to the details of his own historical situatedness and to the relations of power that structure his own discourse (as we saw in our discussion of the "tu quoque" critique at the end of chapter 1), and a difficulty and uneasiness when it comes to justifying his normative political commitments. The biblical great reversal, however, finds a different way through these problems, and we can see it in the treatment of boasting at the end of 1 Corinthians 1.

"So That No Human Being Might Boast" (v. 29)

At the end of Paul's argument about power and wisdom, he makes explicit its immediate implication for his readers:

> God chose what is low and despised in the world, even things that are not, to bring to nothing things that are, so that no human being might boast in the presence of God. And because of him you are in Christ Jesus, who became to us wisdom from God, righteousness and sanctification and redemption, so that, as it is written, "Let the one who boasts, boast in the Lord." (1 Cor. 1:28–31)

This prohibition of boasting in anyone but the Lord addresses a problem similar to the one that Foucault is trying to navigate when he rejects anthropological universals and insists that truth is a "thing of this world." The problem is the self-sufficiency of those who confidently assume that the future will be like the present and that their ruses of wisdom and power will stand the test of time. They are those whom the psalmist has in mind when he says that "some trust in chariots and some in horses" (Ps. 20:7). They may be confident in their endowments, but Paul condemns them with the words, "What do you have that you did not receive? If then you received it, why do you boast as if you did not receive it?" (1 Cor. 4:7).

Within a biblical framework, this boasting plays the same

role that absolute truth and anthropological universals do for Foucault: it creates an illusory and dangerous sense of continuity where there is none. However, whereas Foucault addresses the problem by making truth local and finite, the Bible retains a notion of universal truth, but takes it out of the hands of human beings and builds into it a dynamic that resists and subverts any attempt to use it for self-aggrandizing ends.

First of all, the Bible retains a notion of trans-temporal truth, but takes it out of the hands of human beings. The Lord is the one "declaring the end from the beginning and from ancient times things not yet done, saying, 'My counsel shall stand, and I will accomplish all my purpose,'" (Isa. 46:10). As for human plans:

> Come now, you who say, "Today or tomorrow we will go into such and such a town and spend a year there and trade and make a profit"—yet you do not know what tomorrow will bring. What is your life? For you are a mist that appears for a little time and then vanishes. Instead you ought to say, "If the Lord wills, we will live and do this or that." As it is, you boast in your arrogance. All such boasting is evil. (James 4:13–16)

There are, in other words, anthropological universals, but they do not have their origin in the human mind and cannot be manipulated by human agents. God knows the end from the beginning, but for a human to claim such knowledge is condemnable boasting.

Second, the Bible builds into its notion of truth a dynamic that subverts any attempt to use it for self-aggrandizing ends or for the purpose of claiming self-sufficiency. The universal truth to which Paul appeals in 1 Corinthians 1 is the word of the cross: that Christ (1) gave his life (2) to save his enemies (3) in obedience to his Father. Each of these three elements provides a blueprint of truth that actively militates against the "boasting" that

Paul condemns. This undermines any attempt to use it (1) for building up the self, (2) for privileging one social group over another, or (3) for following one's own agenda.

In sum, Foucault undermines universal truth (an unwarranted projection of the present into the future and the past), but does so at the price of sacrificing a justification for normative ethical or political commitment. 1 Corinthians 1 undermines boasting (an unwarranted projection of the present into the future and the past), but keeps normative justification, doing so in a way that subverts its misappropriation for self-aggrandizing ends. Cruciform wisdom and power, unlike Foucault's casting of truth as "a thing of this world," furnish a robust framework for the sort of normative position that Foucault cannot reach: a position which valorizes normative political commitment, but which also forecloses anthropological universals. To give of oneself to the weak and to those unable to help themselves, to seek harmony with others rather than discord, are positively mandated and given normative weight in both the Philippians 2 passage ("Have this mind among yourselves, which is yours in Christ Jesus," Phil. 2:5) and in 1 Corinthians 1 ("Let the one who boasts, boast in the Lord," 1 Cor. 1:31). What is subverted in these passages is not normative commitment itself (the danger of Foucault's position, which many commentators have grappled with), but the abuse of the possibility of such commitment for ends of self-aggrandizement and violent appropriation of the means to achieve it. Put at its bluntest, the Bible provides a model for dealing with truth in a way that addresses Foucault's concerns without leaving us with his normative problems.

There remains one problem identified by Foucault, however, which I have not yet addressed and which would seem to be compounded by the two biblical passages I have been discussing. It is the question of the ethical priority of self-creation or self-transformation and the way in which universals—be they human or divine—prevent such creativity and act to normalize the process of human subjectivation and shut down many possible creative experiments in living. This objection requires that we turn to consider the question of identity, perhaps the most complex idea around which to weave a conversation between Foucault's position and the biblical great reversal. It is to this important theme that we turn now in the final chapter.

7

CRUCIFORM IDENTITY

The biblical motif of the great reversal that we have been tracing through Philippians 2 and 1 Corinthians 1 also provides the shape of a biblical understanding of identity that we can set alongside Foucault's discussions of the same theme in his later, ethical works. In this chapter, I will seek to elaborate a notion of cruciform identity by returning to 1 Corinthians 1 and supplementing it with reference to other biblical passages and to Augustine's *Confessions*.

Closed and Open Identities

We saw above (chapter 3) how Foucault presents two contrasting accounts of the subject. The first is of normalized identities, heteronomously controlled and closed to self-transformation.

Following in the footsteps of Sade and Bataille, the second is a subject destabilized by limit-experience in a way that opens it to transformation. It is an open identity, compared to the closed identity of normalization.

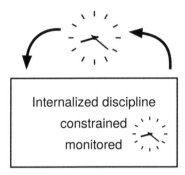

Fig. 7.1. The Normalized Subject.

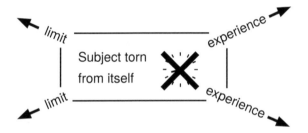

Fig. 7.2. The Destabilized Subject of Limit-Experience.

From a biblical point of view, however, we might query whether this is really a fracturing of the subject at all, rather than a way of traveling the same linear road of closure by other means. Foucault's figures of liminality and exclusion, such as madness, criminality, and proliferating sexual pleasures and practices, provide a very domestic vision of openness and transcendence, compared with the qualitative otherness of God to his creation.

1 Corinthians 1 and the Opening of Subjectivity

The biblical v-shaped dynamic that we have been discussing in these pages also fractures the controlled, normalized subject, doing so in a way that opens it to this radical, divine alterity. We can appreciate how this fracturing works by revisiting the language of 1 Corinthians 1.

The normalized subject runs in the tramlines of the canons of thought and linear power narratives of the age: wisdom and power are attained by progressively seeking their linear increase. This "boastful subject" (as we might call it, using the language of 1 Corinthians 1) is a closed loop: it knows what it must do in order to be wise and powerful, it knows that wisdom and power are in its grasp if only it exerts enough effort, and it strives in a linear way to achieve those desired ends. To the extent that it achieves wisdom and power, it can boast in its own achievement. It is a subject whose goals, achievement, and boasting all circle back to itself: it is self-contained.

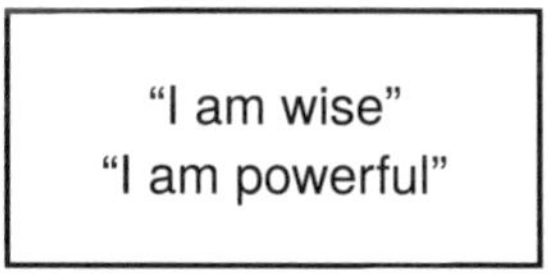

> "I am wise"
> "I am powerful"

Fig. 7.3. The Boastful Subject: Self-Contained.

This closure of the self upon itself is fractured by an encounter with the foolishness and the weakness of "the word of the cross," for, as we have seen, no self-sufficient or closed notions of wisdom and power can pass through the cross without being broken down and rebuilt differently, with God's wisdom and knowledge at the center. Such an encounter with the cross is described in terms of a radical transformation of the self:

> I have been crucified with Christ. It is no longer I who live, but Christ who lives in me. And the life I now live in the flesh I live by faith in the Son of God, who loved me and gave himself for me. (Gal. 2:20; see also Rom. 6:3–5; 2 Cor. 5:17)

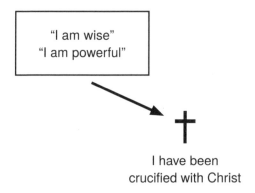

Fig. 7.4. The cross fractures the closed, boastful self.

What emerges from an encounter with the cross is a self that is fractured and open to otherness at its deepest level, a truth beautifully captured by Augustine in his *Confessions*, in the line already quoted above in which he addresses God as "interior intimo meo et superior summo meo" (higher than my highest and more inward than my innermost self).[1] Again, in *De Magistro*, Augustine maintains that "our real Teacher is he who is . . . listened to, who is said to dwell in the inner man, namely Christ."[2]

Also, and crucially, the cruciform self recasts self-knowledge as "doxological dispossession," a term coined by Michael Hanby in *Augustine and Modernity* to describe Augustine's experience in the *Confessions*.[3] According to Augustine, his self is dispersed and scattered; he only experiences something approaching a coherent sense of self when he reaches beyond himself in praise of God, when "by him I may apprehend in whom I have been

---

1. Augustine, *Confessions*, 3.6.11.

2. Augustine, "The Teacher," in *Augustine: Earlier Writings*, ed. John H. S. Burleigh (Philadelphia: Westminster Press, 1953), 95. Augustine is referring to Ephesians 3:16–17.

3. Michael Hanby, *Augustine and Modernity* (London: Routledge, 2003), 289.

apprehended, and may be gathered together again from my for-mer days."⁴ For Augustine, the question is how an always already fractured self can gather itself, the answer being that it can do so only by reaching beyond itself to God.

It is impossible to close the circle of self-identity in a way that excludes the infinite involvement and initiative of God, a truth that Paul joyfully acknowledges when he speaks of his own identity:

> For I am the least of the apostles, unworthy to be called an apostle, because I persecuted the church of God. But by the grace of God I am what I am, and his grace toward me was not in vain. On the contrary, I worked harder than any of them, though it was not I, but the grace of God that is with me. (1 Cor. 15:9–10)

The ineliminable centrality of the grace of God prevents Paul's identity from ever becoming a closed feedback loop of self-assertion.

The cruciform self is not fractured only by this introduc-tion of otherness at its very core, however, but also in two addi-tional ways. First of all, the closed self is fractured by the way in which cruciform identity is thrown outside itself in imitation of the self-giving that characterized Christ's death. Second, it is opened by the new dynamic of boasting: not now a closed loop of self-congratulation, but boasting "in the Lord" (1 Cor. 1:31), which opens the self to otherness of God at the moment of its deepest affirmation of identity.

This openness of self-giving entails a self-forgetfulness which exposes self-abnegation and self-assertion as mirror images of each other, trapped in the same self-focus, as John Milbank points

---

4. Augustine, *Confessions*, 11.29, quoted by Hanby, *Augustine and Modernity*, 24.

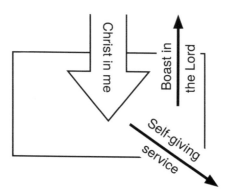

Fig. 7.5. The Open Cruciform Self.

out: "The subject totally preoccupied with the management of its own desiring energies, with their suppression, or else their liberation, is the subject engendered by disciplinary practices."[5] So whichever way it turns, the cruciform self has no closure upon itself, no insularity either from the radical otherness of God or from the relative otherness of neighbor.

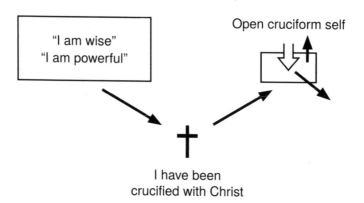

Fig. 7.6. The cross fractures the closed, boastful self.

5. John Milbank, *Theology and Social Theory: Beyond Secular Reason*, 2nd ed. (Oxford: Blackwell, 2006), 294.

Another Look at Openness and Closure

In addition to juxtaposing Foucault's and the Bible's accounts of fractured or open subjectivity, it is worth thinking for a moment about the opposition between closure and openness itself. The way in which I have been presenting the distinction so far makes it look as though the key difference is between openness and closure as such, with the closed, normalized subject opposed to the open, self-transforming subject toward which Foucault gestures in his essay on the limit-experience:

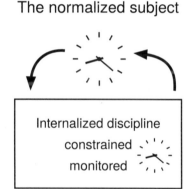

The normalized subject

Internalized discipline

constrained

monitored

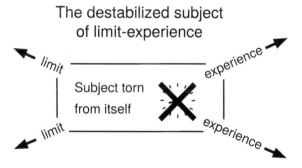

The destabilized subject
of limit-experience

limit — experience

Subject torn
from itself

limit — experience

Fig. 7.7. **The normalized subject and the subject of limit-experience seem to be opposed on the question of openness and closure.**

This, however, is a truncated picture of what is at stake in Foucault's account of the limit-experience. Underlying both the closed, normalized subject and the openness which Foucault opposes to it are divergent visions of the good that motivate and serve to justify the moves made by the respective accounts of the subject.

- The closed, normalized subject reflects an idea of the good that places a high value on stability, conformity, and order, and it negatively values disorder and anarchy.
- Foucault's fractured subject, open to transformation, conforms to a vision according to which the good is identified with autonomous creativity, diversity, and self-expression, and where unthinking conformity is negatively valued.

At this level of the underlying notions of the good, the difference is not in fact between openness and closure at all, but between two positive visions which act as norms controlling the respective accounts of subjectivity to which they give rise (see Fig. 7.8).

Understood at this level, "openness" is just as normalizing and exclusive as "closure": it must necessarily exclude closure and constraint in order to conform to its own norm of openness and freedom. The vision of the good that underpins the transgressive subject of transformation is itself not open to transformation and cannot be transgressed. Furthermore, it is necessary that it be closed in this way, lest the subject cease to be a subject of transformation after all. What is at stake in these two moments of subjectivity is not a distinction between norm and lack of norm, but a question of which norm is to be preferred, and this can only be arbitrated at the level of the visions of the good that underlie the two pictures of subjectivity.

The important question, at this point, becomes how we might account for the origin of these different norms, and specifically

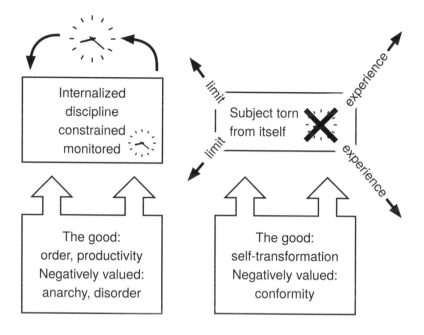

Fig. 7.8. Both the normalized subject and the destabilized subject of limit-experience conform to a vision of the good.

whether an account of their origin stands in tension with their own expression. It is to that question that we now turn in our final reflection on the theme of identity in Foucault.

Autonomous and Heteronomous Identities

There is one further thread of Foucauldian thought that I wish to follow before constraints of space require me to bring this book to a close. Central to Foucault's insistence on self-transformation is, precisely, that it is *self*-transformation: the askesis that Foucault discusses favorably in his later work is "a training of oneself by oneself" (*FR*, 364), and "the principle of an autonomy and sovereignty of self over self" was "the crowning achievement of this effort and work of ancient askesis" (*LCF-CT*,

132n). While not excluding guidance from a spiritual director, it is essential to such ascetic practice that it be autonomous.

The autonomy of the self in crafting its individual askesis is central to Foucault's account of subjectivation and also to his politics. Surely, one might think, this stands in stark contrast to a biblical paradigm of heteronomous transformation by another. Without seeking to deny for a moment that there is an important difference between how Foucault envisions self-transformation and the cruciform self of the Bible, I want to show in this final section that the two are not as far apart as they may appear, and that it is inadequate either to describe Foucault's self-transformation as autonomous or the cruciform self as heteronomous.

Foucault, Transformation, and Autonomy

Foucault's ethic of self-transformation requires a self to do the transforming, a self that is not merely the effect of discourses and power relations that are exterior to it. Such a self, we have seen, is available to Foucault, caught up as it is in the flows and resistances of power. The question I want to ask is not whether the agent of transformation can be the autonomous self (for it seems reasonable to conclude that it can), but how, on Foucault's terms, we can know that any particular transformation or desire for transformation is an autonomous action or desire.

Let us be clear: the proposition to which Foucault is being summoned to respond here is not that we are certain that at every point the "self" we experience as acting autonomously is a symptom of power relations in the face of which it is overwhelmingly passive, but that we can never be certain at what points it is acting autonomously and at what points it is such a symptom. The question is an epistemological one. Furthermore, if the origin of transformation cannot be guaranteed to be autonomous, then there is no way of knowing whether what is construed as "self-transformation" is what it claims to be or whether it is rather the effect of conditioning by social forces and relations of power that are acting upon it from the outside. To be a little more concrete, let us take as an example the imperative "Transform yourself!" Such an imperative can circulate within a particular society and exercise a normalizing function, just as much as the command "Conform!" If I live in a society which finds a hundred subtle ways a day to send me the message "Conform!" and I do conform, then I can hardly claim to be following my own initiative. Similarly, if I live in a society which finds a hundred subtle ways a day to send me the message "Transform yourself!" and I determine to transform myself, then am I not in the same position as the conformist in a society of conformity? Let us represent the problem pictorially. It is impossible to guarantee that I can tell the difference between this:

Fig. 7.9. Autonomous Self-Transformation.

and this:

Fig. 7.10. Pseudo-Autonomous Self-Transformation.

If I seek to transform myself within a culture that is telling me to transform myself (or, equally, if I seek conformity and stability within a culture in which the vision of the good promotes those values), I am epistemologically unable to trace the origin of that injunction, on pain of taking a God's-eye position outside my own situatedness. My desires and ambitions may be real enough to me, but that is not the question. The question is whether, in their origin, they are autonomous or hetoronomous. Am I doing and desiring what I want, or am I doing and desiring what I have been conditioned to think I want? Recognizing or reaffirming what I want will not help me to decide that particular question. Am I writing my own story or conforming to the ambient cultural narrative? Indeed, what sense can that distinction have in the first place, and therefore what is the "self" of self-transformation other than, at best, a wing and a prayer or, at worst, a puppet show and a hollow signifier?

The dilemma is strictly undecidable because any way in which I seek to answer the question of whether it is "really me" that desires to transform myself is always already implicated in the same undecidability it seeks to arbitrate. In other words, I cannot bootstrap my way out of not being able to verify the autonomy of my will. The risk run by Foucault's account of openness—and it is a risk that is impossible to eliminate—is that the self-transforming subject is recycling stale cultural commonplaces in a way that appears creative and appears to provide an opening into genuine otherness, but that, even in its very desire for the new and for otherness itself, amounts to a parroting of ambient cultural norms, including the cultural norm of seeking and privileging the new.

So under two seemingly opposite accounts of the subject (as "open" and "closed"), we have discerned two normalizing visions of the good, and we can now see that these two accounts of subjectivity are united in a common dilemma as to the origin of their respective visions of the good. The two positions alike eventually have to resort to some variant of the dogmatic assertion "I just know that I know," or have to live with the uncertainty of autonomy and heteronomy without being able to resolve it. Both encounter the same problem: neither "open" nor "closed" subjectivity can give an account of itself that allows us to isolate a moment of autonomy within it. Any appeal to the self or to agency is always on the verge of collapsing into the heteronomy from which it would seek to distinguish itself. When we turn to cruciform identity, however, we can elaborate an approach that avoids this dilemma because, in its fractured openness to the infinite, triune God, it does not exist between the poles of autonomy and heteronomy in the first place, as I shall now seek to explain.

The Cruciform Self and Heteronomy

In the discussion of symmetry and asymmetry above (chapter 5), I argued that we cannot account for the cruciform self in the binary terms of autonomy and heteronomy. The relation of God's agency to the Christian's initiative is not that of "action upon the action of others," for I exist only through his ongoing act of upholding me (and everything else in the universe) "by the word of his power" (Heb. 1:3). The Bible holds together divine sovereignty and human responsibility in a way that compromises neither. This would of course be impossible with a human-human relationship, but we must not think of the relation of God to one of his creatures according to the pattern of the relationship between two creatures. If we did, we could never make sense of verses like Philippians 2:12–13: "Work out your own salvation with fear and trembling, *for* it is God who works in you, both to will and to work for his good pleasure." The "for" here translates the even starker Greek *gar*, "indeed." The only biblical way to answer the question "Is God working here, or the Christian?" is "Yes, and yes."

We can now see how this picture is further complicated in the case of cruciform identity, because when I give myself to God, I am inhabited and transformed by a new indwelling presence, the Spirit of Christ: "For the desires of the flesh are against the Spirit, and the desires of the Spirit are against the flesh, for these are opposed to each other, to keep you from doing the things you want to do" (Gal. 5:17). This further develops the reflections above on Foucault's characterization of Christianity as a religion of renunciation. Reducing the cruciform dynamic to renunciation alone assumes a closed and unchangeable rigidity of desire, a picture that is contested by the biblical witness. The self and its desires are complicated in the Christian, for the "desires of the Spirit" come and oppose the "desires of the flesh" in a way that makes the Christian ethical experience nonlinear. If we adopt the language of Galatians 5, to renounce the flesh is to embrace and satisfy one's desire for the Spirit, and to satisfy the flesh is to renounce the Spirit. The choice is not over whether to renounce, but what to renounce.

In addition to calling into question the motif of renunciation, the intimate sustaining, indwelling, and transforming of the Christian by God that we explored above in relation to Augustine means that the autonomy/heteronomy dyad is inadequate to describe the complex relational dynamics at play in cruciform identity. Biblical language bursts the I/you dichotomy when it talks of the relation between the Christian and Christ, transgressing that boundary again and again:

> I have been crucified with Christ. It is no longer I who live, but Christ who lives in me. And the life I now live in the flesh I live by faith in the Son of God, who loved me and gave himself for me. (Gal. 2:20)

I propose, therefore, to introduce the rather unwieldy term "theautonomy" (from *theos*, "God," and *autos*, "self") to describe such a complex identity that cannot be reduced to the poles of autonomy and heteronomy (nor to a theonomy, in which the Christian would be the mere puppet of God). The idea that "theautonomy" is trying to communicate is that the *theos* and the *autos* cannot be neatly extricated from each other: God is not an alien agency acting upon the autonomous individual.

Theautonomy (understood in this sense) diagonalizes the difference between autonomy and heteronomy because God is neither myself nor a distinct fellow creature; I am not him, nor can I exist independently of him, and he is "higher than my highest and more inward than my innermost self." Theautonomy bursts open the categories of autonomy and heteronomy.

Fig. 7.11. Biblical anthropology confounds the distinction between autonomy and heteronomy.

How does this paradigm of the cruciform self address the dilemma that haunts Foucault's ethic of self-transformation? That dilemma, it will be remembered, is epistemological: I can never determine on my own whether the way that I am acting or what I am desiring is the result of my own initiative or of an ambient cultural norm to which I find myself conforming, all the while assuming that I am acting on my own initiative. There are two answers. The first has to do with what has been called the "absolute personality theism" of the Bible.[6] God is personal, not impersonal, so the personal goes all the way down and all the way back in the universe. Only such an account of personality, the argument goes, can guarantee the integrity and agency of persons within creation as images of the absolute, triune personal agency of God.[7] The second answer has to do with the idea of revelation. The problem for Foucault is that I can never think about my own thinking or my own willing from the outside in a way that would provide for me a non-question-begging witness about my own agency. To the question "When I think that I am transforming myself, is it really my initiative?" the only answer Foucault can offer is the circular "I think so." By contrast, the Bible, in its own terms, provides just such a word from outside my own thinking—and, crucially, from outside creation—that underwrites the meaningfulness of my will in the context of the will of God:

> As Christians we hold that determinate human experience could work to no end, could work in accordance with no plan, and could not even get under way, if it were not for the existence of the absolute will of God. It is on this ground then that

6. See, for example, John Frame, *The Doctrine of God* (Phillipsburg, NJ: P&R Publishing, 2002), 25.

7. See my argument about the sovereignty of God and the dignity of human choices in the Derrida volume in this series.

we hold to the absolute will of God as the presupposition of the will of man. Looked at in this way, that which to many seems at first glance to be the greatest hindrance to moral responsibility, namely the conception of an absolutely sovereign God, becomes the very foundation of its possibility.[8]

What we have seen in this final chapter is that biblical, cruciform identity provides a series of resources for addressing the concerns and problems that Foucault raises, and it does so in ways that are, in the specific ways discussed, more complex and deeper than his own responses. The openness which he seeks to secure for identity through the fracturing of the limit-experience has been compared to the manifold openness of the cruciform self, and the epistemological impossibility of validating autonomy over heteronomy for Foucault has been shown not to be a problem for the biblical account, which surpasses those rigid categories.

8. Cornelius Van Til, *Christian Theistic Evidences* (Phillipsburg, NJ: Presbyterian and Reformed Publishing Company, 1978), 83.

8

CONCLUSION: JEWS DEMAND SIGNS, GREEKS SEEK WISDOM, AND FOUCAULT . . .

The aim of this book has not been to adjudicate between Foucault and the Bible on the question of truth. Such a verdict would rest on whether there is, for example, something like the Creator-creature distinction or not, and such questions take us far beyond the scope of these brief pages. My aim has been more modest: to draw out and compare Foucauldian and biblical approaches to some key themes that are important to both parties in the conversation.

This is not the whole story, however. I stressed in the introduction that any engagement between Foucault and the Bible must respect the type of writing that Foucault offers us. In other words, the method of comparison must respect Foucault's form, as well as his content. It will not have escaped the attentive reader's notice, I am sure, that I have been seeking to abide by this principle in my reading of the Bible, as well as in my treatment of

Foucault. In fact, the great reversal, particularly in its expression in 1 Corinthians 1, has provided not only the content of the foregoing analysis, but also much of its form as well. Following Paul's engagement with Greek and Jewish culture, I have sought to discern what Foucault wants or values, to show how he proposes to attain it, and to compare his approach with biblical passages that address similar concerns. A pattern has emerged in these analyses:

1. Foucault's goals (such as a history of ruptures, an account of power that goes beyond the simplistic paradigm of monarchical, sovereign rule, an open account of identity, and a refusal of anthropological universals) very often correspond to biblical motifs and values.
2. But the ways in which he seeks to reach those goals preclude consideration of a biblical approach.
3. The goals can be more comprehensively achieved if pursued within a biblical framework, although this requires them to be dismantled and rebuilt at the foot of the cross.

This, of course, follows Paul's schema in 1 Corinthians 1:

1. "For Jews demand signs and Greeks seek wisdom."
2. "But we preach Christ crucified, a stumbling block to Jews and folly to Gentiles."
3. "For the foolishness of God is wiser than men, and the weakness of God is stronger than men."

If the Greeks seek true wisdom, then they must embrace the foolish cross; if the Jews seek true power, then they must embrace the weakness and the offense of the cross. If Foucault seeks a radical transformation of the self, then he must leave behind the control inherent in the "self-" of self-transformation and abandon himself to the only radically other who can open the self to a noncircular transformation at the deepest level.

This is not meant to sound like a cute theological "gotcha"; it seeks to respect the shape of biblical thinking, as well as its content. There are, to be sure, Foucauldian responses to be made to this approach, and I make no claim that the present book represents the final word in the conversation between Foucault and the Bible. Quite the contrary: the present volume is the *amuse bouche* at a dinner party that, like Plato's banquet, can stretch late into the night and include multiple rounds of statement and reply. It is my hope that the cruciform method of analysis that I have followed in these pages has ventriloquized neither Foucault nor the Bible, and that it can help others to strike up new conversations between the Bible and other philosophers far beyond the scope of the present volume or the expertise of its author.

APPENDIX 1: FOUCAULT'S MAIN PUBLICATIONS

Title	Period/phase	Subject	Key notions/figures	Striking opening image/idea	Surprising conclusion
Folie et déraison: Histoire de la folie à l'âge classique (1961) [Madness and Civilization: A History of Insanity in the Age of Reason, 1965 (heavily abridged edition). History of Madness, 2006 (unabridged)]	Pre-archaeology	On the ruptures in the understanding of madness from the end of the medieval period to the modern day.	Renaissance: the ship of fools; Classical age: the great confinement, reason, animality; the modern age: the age of the asylum, Pinel and Tuke, Freud.	stultifera navis (the ship of fools).	Releasing the mentally ill from madhouses is not merely a humanitarian gesture.
Naissance de la clinique: Une archéologie du regard médical (1963) [The Birth of the Clinic: An Archaeology of Medical Perception, 1973]	Pre-archaeology	The transformation in the understanding of disease and the clinic in the move from the Classical to the modern age.	Epistemological rupture between the Classical clinic (disease exists independently of its symptoms) and the modern clinic (the body is examined to reveal the severity of the disease). The medical gaze. Bichat.	"Towards the middle of the eighteenth century, Pomme treated and cured a hysteric by making her take baths, ten or twelve whole hours a day, for ten whole months."	The modern clinic was born in an epistemological rupture at the end of the eighteenth century.
Les mots et les choses (1966) [The Order of Things, 1970]	Archaeology	On the emergence of the human sciences.	Three epistemes: Renaissance (resemblance), Classical (representation), modern (limits of representation, emergence of "man").	Velázquez, Las Meninas; Borges on Chinese classification.	"Man is an invention of recent date. And one perhaps nearing its end."
L'archéologie du savoir (1969) [Archaeology of Knowledge, 2002]	Archaeology	Foucault's most theoretical work, seeking to explain the method of archaeology.	Discourse. Discursive formations (rather than epistemes). The archive. Enunciative modalities; strategies. Historical a priori. Moving from archaeology to genealogy.		Our economics, social practices, mythology, and stories are governed by rules not all given to our consciousness.

Title	Period/phase	Subject	Key notions/figures	Striking opening image/idea	Surprising conclusion
Surveiller et punir: Naissance de la prison (1975) [*Discipline and Punish: The Birth of the Prison*, 1977]	Genealogy (first full-length and most advanced genealogy)	The changes in modes of punishment from the Classical to the modern age.	Sovereignty/sovereign power. Disciplinary power. The Panopticon. Micro-physics of power. Docile bodies. Normalization.	The torture of Damiens, the regicide.	The end of public torture is not due to an increased humanitarianism. Power isn't just something outside us that we need to resist.
Histoire de la sexualité, vol. 1: *La volonté de savoir* (1976) [*The History of Sexuality*, vol. 1: *The Will to Knowledge*, 1978]	Genealogy	The emergence of new categories of sexuality in the nineteenth century, and how those categories developed.	The repressive hypothesis. Discursive explosion. The hysterical woman, the masturbating child, the perverse adult, and the Malthusian couple. Confession. Biopower/biopolitics. Normalization.	The repressive hypothesis misunderstands both Victorian and contemporary discourse on sexuality.	We have misunderstood sexual "liberation."
Histoire de la sexualité, vol. 2: *L'usage des plaisirs* (1984) [*The History of Sexuality*, vol. 2: *The Use of Pleasure*, 1985]	Ethics (his interest begins in 1981)	Sex in Greek antiquity.	Greek sexuality. Care of the self. Mode of subjectivation. The use of pleasures. Problematization. Ascetics. Biopower.		
Histoire de la sexualité, vol. 3: *Le souci de soi* (1984) [*The History of Sexuality*, vol. 3: *The Care of the Self*, 1986]	Ethics	Sex in Roman antiquity.	Aphrodisia. The care of the self.		

APPENDIX 2: FOUCAULT'S PERIODIZATIONS

	Christian/Medieval	Renaissance	Classical	Modern	Postmodern
		From 1400s Florence to early 17th century	From Descartes to Kant: roughly 1650 to 1800	Nineteenth century	
The Order of Things		Resemblance, analogy, similitude. Correspondences between things: aconite.	Representation. Taxonomy and mathematical classification. Not similitude, but variation and measurement.	Not representation, but interpretation. Not mathesis and taxonomia, but analysis. Birth of linguistics, economics, and the life sciences. "Man" is both subject and object of investigation. Kant thinks that representation is just one form of thought among others.	Structure
		Cervantes's *Don Quixote*—sign and signifier separate			
			Kant: representation is not neutral. It has a history.		
			Sade is the end of classicism.		
			Velázquez's *Las Meninas* between the Classical and the modern ages		
			Manet undoes representation.		
				Klee challenges the separation of linguistic and visual signs (+ Magritte in The *Treachery of Images*, an "unlimited interplay" of word and image).	
				Kandinsky picks apart the assumption that resemblance implies affirmation.	
				First adumbrations of postmodernism in Nietzsche (end of *OT*).	
		Words are things and participate in the same resemblances/ similitudes as other things.	Language is external to things. It does not constitute them, but explains them: general grammar.	Language is an object. Also an intensification of literary language. Back to language as autonomous: linguistics.	
History of Madness	No distinct identity or place	The ship of fools. The wisdom of the Shakespearean fool; madness as apocalyptic warning.	The great confinement.	The age of the asylum.	
			Pinel and Tuke.		
Power (including Discipline and Punish)	Pastoral power	Sovereign power.	Disciplinary power/biopower.	Biopower/disciplinary power.	
			The intention of the military rifle.		

GLOSSARY

Absolute personality theism. A theme in volume 2 of Hermann Bavinck's *Reformed Dogmatics*, taken up by Cornelius Van Til and further developed by John Frame, according to which the biblical revelation of God is distinguished from other religions by the claim that God is both absolute and personal, and that these two fundamental truths about God are equally ultimate and not in conflict with one another.

Age of the asylum. In *History of Madness*, the period that begins with the penal reforms of Philippe Pinel and Samuel Tuke in the late eighteenth and early nineteenth centuries and comes to an end at the beginning of the twentieth century with the psychoanalysis that removes the mad from the asylum and places them on the analyst's couch. See also: great confinement; Pinel, Philippe; Tuke, Samuel.

Anthropological universal. A term to describe those categories of human behavior that are taken—falsely, according to Foucault—to remain invariant over time and location. Examples of such false universals from Foucault's own work include "madness" and "sexuality." See also: historical a priori.

Archaeology. Foucault's method in his books of the 1960s, referred to explicitly in *The Order of Things* and *Archaeology of Knowledge* and found in nascent form in *History of Madness* and *The Birth of the Clinic*. As opposed to conventional academic histories, Foucault's archaeologies (1) are not concerned with individual experience, (2) do not see historical change as the result of human agency, but of changes in concepts, and (3) see history not as a continuous progression, but as a series of ruptures. Archaeology explores, not the history of particular events, but of the conditions necessary for certain events to take place. See also: ethics; genealogy.

Archive. A term used by Foucault in *Archaeology of Knowledge*. An archive is the "the first law of what can be said, the system that governs the appearance of statements as unique events" (*AK*, 129), establishing the rules of what is sayable and thinkable at a given historical moment. As such, it sits between the rules of language (which allow, in principle, an infinite number of statements) and the corpus of all the statements which in fact have been made. Foucault maintains that it is impossible for us to describe our own archive (*AK*, 30).

Askesis. A transliteration of the Greek *askēsis*, which means "exercise" or "training," askesis is the discipline of "testing oneself, examining oneself, monitoring oneself in a series of clearly defined exercises" (*HS3*, 68). It encompasses a wide variety of historical practices from ancient Greek self-formation through Christian spiritual exercises to the "homosexual askesis that would make us work on ourselves and invent, I do not say discover, a manner of being that is still improbable" (*FL*, 206).

Augustine of Hippo. 354–430. Church father and author of *Confessions* and *The City of God*. Augustine's insistence on the primacy of love has been compared to Foucault's focus on the notion of power, and his account of the dispersed self being gathered as it reaches beyond itself in praise of God is used in the present volume as a contrast to Foucault's fracturing of the subject in limit-experiences.

Autonomy. From the Greek *autos* (self) and *nomos* (law), the idea that the self gives itself its own (ethical and behavioral) laws, as opposed to these laws being dictated by another. See also: heteronomy.

Bachelard, Gaston. 1884–1962. French philosopher of science famous, along with Georges Canguilhem, for the notion of the "epistemological break" in the history of science. See also: Canguilhem, Georges; epistemological break.

Bataille, Georges. 1897–1962. French philosopher and author in whose writing extreme erotic and violent content serves a mystical, spiritual end. Foucault wrote on Bataille's work in "A Preface to Transgression" (*LCP*, 29–52), and Bataille influenced Foucault's understanding of the importance of limit-experience. See also: Blanchot, Maurice; limit-experience; Nietzsche, Friedrich; Sade, Marquis de.

Biopolitics. In Foucault's later work, a term to describe the forces which "brought life and its mechanisms into the realm of explicit calculations and made knowledge-power an agent of transformation of human life" (*HS1*, 143). Given the imperative to provide sufficient soldiers to supply a standing army, biopolitical considerations arose in the West in the eighteenth and nineteenth centuries and extend to the increased monitoring of the health of individuals and populations in this period, as well as to the way in which capitalism disciplines bodies to extract from them the maximum yield for the minimum effort.

Biopower. Like many of Foucault's terms, biopower receives a number of different meanings in his work. In *STP*, he defines it as "the set of mechanisms through which basic biological features of the human species became the object of a political strategy" (*LCF-STP*, 1). As opposed to disciplinary power, it treats whole populations, not individuals. As opposed to the sovereign power which Foucault characterizes as "the right to *take* life or *let* live" (*HS1*, 138, emphasis original), biopower is "a power to *foster* life or *disallow* it to the point of death" (*HS1*, 138, emphasis original). See also: disciplinary power; heterosexuality; pastoral power; sovereign power.

Blanchot, Maurice. 1907–2003. French author and literary theorist who, along with Sade, Bataille, and Nietzsche, influenced Foucault's understanding of the limit-experience. See also: Bataille, Georges; limit-experience; Nietzsche, Friedrich; Sade, Marquis de.

Canguilhem, Georges. Philosopher and historian of science responsible, along with Gaston Bachelard, for the influential notion of the "epistemological break," or rupture, in the history of science. See also: Bachelard, Gaston; epistemological break.

Capillary power. A term Foucault contrasts to centralized, sovereign power. Like the system of many tiny capillaries in the body, from which it draws its name, capillary power is diffused over many microrelationships and has no single center, forming what Foucault calls a "micro-physics" of power.

Carceral society. A term not used by Foucault himself, who writes instead of the "carceral system" or "carceral circle." It describes a trend according to which the practices of observation and normalization typical of the modern prison are extended to characterize society in general.

Care of the self. The practical activity Foucault identifies in Stoic and Epicurean thought according to which the individual has a responsibility to intensify his sense of self and to cultivate a "certain mode of being" (*EW1-EST*, 282). See also: ethics.

Cervantes, Miguel de. 1547–1616. Spanish author of *Don Quixote*, which Foucault situates in *The Order of Things* at the rupture between the Renaissance and Classical ages.

Classical age/episteme. The period of Western history running roughly from Descartes's *cogito* to Kant's first *Critique*, during which knowledge is expressed in terms of representation, taxonomy, and measurement, and language is considered to be external to things. It is the period of the great confinement in *History of Madness*. See also: modern era/episteme; Renaissance era/episteme.

Confession. The Christian practice of talking about one's deepest desires with a spiritual guide. Foucault argues that the practice of confession constructs, rather than reveals, the self, and that it has become a generalized condition of late twentieth-century society, present in the domains of psychoanalysis, education, law, and medicine.

Damiens, Robert-François. 1715–57. Convicted of attempted regicide in 1757, Damiens's gruesome torture and execution serves as a vivid illustration of sovereign power at the beginning of *Discipline and Punish*. See also: sovereign power.

Descartes, René. 1596–1650. French philosopher and scientist whose phrase *cogito ergo sum* ("I am thinking, therefore I exist") epitomizes for Foucault the paradigm of representation characteristic of the Classical age.

Desire. A term of which Foucault is increasingly suspicious in the 1970s, on the grounds that it implies a lack and a longing for an absent object. He prefers "pleasure," which he understands to create its objects, rather than mourn their absence.

Diagonalization. A term used in this book (and also in *Thinking* *through Creation* and the *Derrida* volume in this series) to describe the way in which one way of thinking treats an either/or choice offered by another way of thinking as a false dichotomy, refusing to be bound by the assumptions and categories offered to it. To diagonalize is neither to embrace wholeheartedly nor to reject outright, but to rearrange and recategorize concepts in new and unexpected ways, cutting across customary boundaries.

Dialectic. Describes the way in which, according to Hegel, history progresses not in a straightforwardly linear manner, but by a series of sublations (*Aufhebungen*) of seeming contradictions. See also: *Geist*; Hegel, Georg Friedrich Wilhelm.

Dialectical materialism. Karl Marx's reframing of Hegelian ideas about the inevitable progress of history within a resolutely materialist framework, removing Hegel's reliance on *Geist* and making economic forces the primary driver of historical change. See also: dialectic; Hegel, Georg Friedrich Wilhelm; Marx, Karl.

Disciplinary power. A form of power prominent in modern societies, modelled on the military discipline necessary for a well-functioning modern army. Individual bodies are schooled and policed through hierarchical observation, normalizing judgment, and examination, so that they conform to norms of behavior. In *Discipline and Punish*, Foucault contrasts the sovereign power exercised upon Damiens, the suspected regicide, with the disciplinary power expressed in the regimented daily schedule prescribed by Faucher, arguing that, whereas sovereign power punishes the body, disciplinary power punishes and normalizes the soul. See also: biopower; Faucher, Léon; pastoral power; sovereign power.

Discursive explosion. In *The Will to Knowledge*, refers to the proliferation of discourse around sex and sexuality in the Victorian period, necessary for the biopolitical monitoring and regulation of populations. This discursive explosion gives the lie to the repressive hypothesis. See also: heterosexuality; repressive hypothesis.

Episteme. Used in *The Order of Things* and *Archaeology of Knowledge* (and once in *Discipline and Punish*) to describe the often unconscious rules that govern the production of knowledge within a particular discourse or discipline at a particular period in history. Epistemes often stretch across disciplines, with naturalists, economists, and grammarians employing similar paradigms to arrive at very different bodies of knowledge in a particular historical epoch.

Epistemological break. In the history of science pioneered by Gaston Bachelard and Georges Canguilhem, an epistemological break or epistemological rupture is an abrupt historical shift, rather than a smooth progression, that characterizes, for example, the move from Newtonian to Einsteinian physics. Foucault takes the notion of the epistemological break from Bachelard and Canguilhem and broadens its scope from science to many other aspects of society. See also: Bachelard, Gaston; Canguilhem, Georges.

Ethics. The third period of Foucault's writing, after archaeology and genealogy. His ethical period is commonly understood to include his major works of the 1980s: volumes 2 and 3 of his *History of Sexuality*. For Foucault, "ethics" is understood not as a means of distinguishing "good" from "evil," but as a term to describe the relation of the self to itself, the self-formation that subjects a body to a particular regime or set of rules with a view to producing a particular mode of being. See also: archaeology; care of the self; genealogy.

Faucher, Léon. 1803–54. Author of a list of rules for "the House of young prisoners in Paris" (1830s), which Foucault cites at the beginning of *Discipline and Punish* as an example of disciplinary power, in contrast to the torture of the attempted regicide Damiens, which epitomizes sovereign power. See also: disciplinary power.

Freud, Sigmund. 1856–1939. Founder of psychoanalysis. Foucault situates Freud at the end of the age of the asylum, but his methods still represent a means of control and institutionalization of the mad. Along with the rest of psychiatry, psychoanalysis is "a monologue of reason about madness" (*HM*, xxviii) which forces the discourse of madness to conform to its categories, drowning out "the voices of unreason" (*HM*, 511).

Geist. German for "spirit" or "mind." The central concept of Hegel's account of history in *Phenomenology of Spirit.* The term is susceptible of multiple meanings and has often been taken to refer to some sort of transcendent world Spirit, but it is commonly understood today to be referring to a collective consciousness common to all people at a particular historical moment. See also: dialectic; Hegel, Georg Friedrich Wilhelm.

Genealogy. The middle period of Foucault's work, after archaeology and before ethics, roughly spanning the 1970s. Foucault does not provide a comprehensive description of his genealogical method nor of its differences from his archaeology, but certain broad trends can be discerned: (1) whereas archaeology focuses on discourse, genealogy takes a wider look at behavior and society; (2) in genealogy the focus is more explicitly on power relations; (3) genealogy is more overtly political than archaeology, analyzing modes of resistance to dominant power relations. See also: archaeology; ethics.

Great confinement. Describes the incarceration of the mad in the Classical age, shut up in "hospitals general" alongside other "unreasonable" groups including criminals, those without work, and libertines. The great confinement ended with the reforms of Philippe Pinel and Samuel Tuke in the latter decades of the eighteenth century. See also: age of the asylum; Pinel, Philippe; Tuke, Samuel.

Great reversal. A theological term to describe the repeated biblical move, prominent in the teaching of Jesus, of reversing customary expectations of merit and reward. The humble are exalted, and the rich are humbled; strength is found in weakness, and wisdom in foolishness. The epitome of the theme is the death of Christ in shame and weakness being a moment of his glorification and of winning the great victory over death.

Hegel, Georg Friedrich Wilhelm. 1770–1831. German philosopher whose influence on modern thought and society is as great as that of any modern thinker. Hegel's influential philosophy of history retains the notion of history moving toward a goal, but rejects the idea of smooth, linear progression in favor of a dialectic movement which progresses through the sublation (*Aufhebung*) of seemingly contradictory concepts. Hegel's insistence on history as inexorable progress, on the importance of human consciousness, and on the all-encompassing nature of dialectical movement all stand in contrast to Foucault's approach. See also: dialectic; *Geist*.

Heteronomy. The idea that it is another (*heteros*) that gives the self its law (*nomos*). If a self is governed heteronomously, it receives the rules of its behavior from outside itself (from another self or from ambient social norms). See also: autonomy.

Heterosexuality. For Foucault, a category invented in the nineteenth century to designate the norm in relation to which "deviant" sexual identities and practices can be labelled and catalogued, which in turn permitted stricter social control of these behaviors. Foucault argues that the gay lifestyle is a mode of being open to both heterosexuals and homosexuals. See also: biopower; discursive explosion.

Historical a priori. Foucault modifies Immanuel Kant's notion of the a priori, the unchanging, pre-given categories in terms of which we necessarily understand everything in our experience. Unlike Kant, Foucault's focus is not on the conditions of validity for judgments, but on the conditions of reality for statements: what is sayable and understandable in a particular historical age. Foucault maintains that such conditions change from age to age, and so the a priori is irreducibly historical. See also: anthropological universal; Kant, Immanuel; truth.

Homosexuality. A nineteenth-century biopolitical category replacing the older "sodomy." Whereas sodomy designates a form of behavior, homosexuality is a fundamental identity, or, as Foucault says, a "species." Sexuality in general and homosexuality in particular take the place previously occupied by the soul: it is the locus of intelligibility of the individual, their deepest and most inviolable self.

Kant, Immanuel. 1724–1804. Along with Hegel, the most influential philosopher of the modern age. In his *Critique of Pure Reason*, Kant insists that our experience of reality conforms to a priori categories of our understanding, rather than our thoughts conforming to categories that exist in the world outside our minds. For Foucault, this signals the modern problematization of man as both subject and object of knowledge. See also: historical a priori; modern era/episteme.

Limit-experience. A term used by Foucault in a 1978 interview to describe a type of experience present in the work of Nietzsche, Sade, Bataille, and Blanchot. Limit-experiences frequently involve extreme eroticism and/or violence and cause the subject to "reach that point of life which lies as close as possible to the impossibility of living, which lies at the limit or extreme" (*RM*, 27) and disrupts or "tears" the subject from itself, destroying its self-contained character. See also: Bataille, Georges; Blanchot, Maurice; Nietzsche, Friedrich; Sade, Marquis de.

Linear and nonlinear thinking. Terms used in the present volume to differentiate between two understandings of power. In a linear account, the acquisition of power is an unbroken ascent and gradual accumulation, whereas the nonlinear account to be found in Philippians 2 and 1 Corinthians 1 associates self-humbling and self-emptying (Philippians) and weakness and foolishness (1 Corinthians) with God's power. The linear/nonlinear dyad echoes Luther's distinction between the theology of glory and the theology of the cross. See also: Luther, Martin; theologian of glory; theologian of the cross; v-shaped dynamic; x-shaped dynamic.

Luther, Martin. 1483–1546. German theologian and seminal figure in the Protestant Reformation. Luther's distinction in the Heidelberg Disputation of 1518 between "theologians of glory" and "theologians of the cross" informs the present volume's reading of power in the Bible and in Foucault. See also: linear and nonlinear thinking; theologian of glory; theologian of the cross.

Marx, Karl. 1818–83. German philosopher and economist. Transformed Hegel's dialectic of *Geist*'s self-realization in history into his own dialectical materialism, retaining the idea that history has an inevitable course and destiny. See also: dialectical materialism; *Geist*; Hegel, Georg Friedrich Wilhelm.

Modern era/episteme. The period of Western history running roughly from Kant's first *Critique* to Nietzsche, during which knowledge is expressed not as representation (as in the Classical age) but as interpretation. In this period, man emerges clearly as both the subject and the object of investigation, and the position of the observer/knower becomes problematic. Language is considered to be autonomous. In *History of Madness*, it is the age of the asylum. See also: Classical era/episteme; Kant, Immanuel; Renaissance era/episteme.

Nietzsche, Friedrich. 1844–1900. German philosopher who understands history as a series of ruptures, rather than a smooth continuity, and who rejected philosophical universals such as rationality and truth. Both of these aspects of Nietzsche's thought influenced Foucault's own archaeological and genealogical methods. See also: anthropological universals; historical a priori.

Normalization. In *Discipline and Punish*, Foucault argues that discipline involves three elements: hierarchical observation, normalizing judgment, and examination. Normalizing judgment is more prescriptive than the logic of the permitted and the forbidden (characteristic of sovereign power) defining as it does a norm of behavior by comparison with which every other possible behavior is an abnormal deviation. The normalized subject conforms itself to the norm, often under the normalizing judgment of medicine, the law, and society. See also: disciplinary power.

Panopticon. An imaginary prison described by utilitarian philosopher Jeremy Bentham (1748–1832) in which a ring of cells encircle a central observation tower. Lights shining from the tower mean that the inmates never know when they are being observed, so they internalize the gaze of the guards and police themselves. Foucault uses the panopticon in *Discipline and Punish* as a picture of the ubiquitous observation and normalization of the disciplinary society. See also: disciplinary power.

Pastoral power. A mode of power relations introduced into the

West by Christianity, in which a pastor or spiritual guide (usually a local priest) has individual oversight of the souls of his flock. They confess to him their sins and deepest desires, and he provides guidance and instruction. See also: biopower; disciplinary power; sovereign power.

Pinel, Philippe. 1745–1826. French physician famous for freeing the insane inmates of the Bicêtre hospital in Paris from their chains. In *History of Madness*, Foucault rejects the dominant narrative of Pinel as a straightforwardly humanitarian hero. See also: age of the asylum; Tuke, Samuel.

Pleasure. As opposed to desire, which relies on lack (we do not desire what we already have, but only that which we lack), pleasure for Foucault is creative and does not imply absence. The Christian attitude toward sexuality is, for Foucault, a battle against pleasure. Part of Foucault's advocacy for the gay lifestyle is that it "makes ourselves infinitely more susceptible to pleasures" (*EW1-EST*, 137). See also: renunciation.

Power. Foucault is reluctant to define power as such, preferring to collect and synthesize examples of particular forms of power (sovereign, pastoral, disciplinary, biopower). He hardly ever uses the word "power" by itself, and when he does use the term, "it is simply as shorthand for the expression I generally use: relations of power" (*EW1-EST*, 291). Foucault does, nevertheless, offer the understanding of power as "action upon the action of others" (*EW3-P*, 345–46). See also: biopower; disciplinary power; pastoral power; sovereign power.

Renaissance era/episteme. The period of Western history running roughly from 1400s Florence to the early 17th century, during which knowledge was expressed in terms of resemblance, analogy, and correspondences between objects and ideas, and when systems of resemblance were thought to embrace not only objects, but also words. In *History of Madness,* it is the period during which madness is considered as an apocalyptic warning. See also: Classical era/episteme; modern era/episteme.

Renunciation. Christian ethics is characterized for Foucault by an ascetic renunciation of the self, of the body, and of pleasure. The goal of confession, he argues, is the renunciation of that which has been disclosed. It forms part of what Foucault calls the "complete renunciation" to God or a spiritual guide: in Christianity, there is "no truth about the self without a sacrifice of the self" (ABHS, 222). See also: pleasure.

Repressive hypothesis. The theory according to which the Victorians spoke very little about sex and sexuality, which Foucault is at pains in *The Will to Knowledge* to reject with his insistence on the nineteenth-century "discursive explosion" around the theme of sex. See also: discursive explosion.

Ressentiment. A term used by Nietzsche in the *Genealogy of Morality* and elsewhere to characterise the prevailing Christian (and Western) ethic. *Ressentiment,* a term close to, but not identical with, resentment, is the attitude of the weak to the strong, bearing a grudge against their strength and at the same time making a virtue of their own weakness, so that they can stand in judgment of the strong.

Sade, Marquis de. 1740–1814. French aristocratic libertine author. Foucault situates Sade's writing on the cusp of the modern era because of the way in which it stretches and pushes at the limits of the capacity of language to represent reality, in Sade's case the reality of sexual frenzy and ecstasy. See also: Bataille, Georges; Blanchot, Maurice; limit-experience; Nietzsche, Friedrich.

Sartre, Jean-Paul. 1905–1980. Existentialist philosopher of post-war France whose approach is at loggerheads with Foucault's on the question of the centrality of the subject and the shape of history. Although they did campaign together on social issues, Sartre and Foucault were hostile to each other intellectually. Sartre accused Foucault's histories of replacing "cinema with a slide show, movement with a succession of immobile structures," and Foucault judged that Sartre's *Critique of Dialectical Reason* was "the magnificent and pathetic attempt by a man of the nineteenth century to think in the twentieth century."

Sovereign power. The mode of power relations dominant in the political sphere in Europe until the rise of disciplinary power in the modern age. Power resides in the body of a sovereign (usually, but not necessarily, a monarch), and any attempt on the life of the sovereign is an attack on the very fabric and order of society. The sovereign has the right to take life (through conscription into the army or by decree) or to let live. See also: biopower; Damiens, Robert-François; disciplinary power; pastoral power; sovereign power.

Subjectivation. The process by which, according to Foucault, a subject or self forms or constitutes itself. A subject is formed through subjection to a particular rule, whether the rule be the ancient Greek ideal of self-fashioning and self-mastery, the more austere Roman self-fashioning, Christian submission to divine law, Classical/modern subjugation to the dictates of reason, or to practices of medical and psychological self-knowledge and identity politics.

Theologian of glory. Luther's term in the Heidelberg Disputation of 1518 for the theologian who "looks upon the invisible things of God as though they were clearly perceptible in those things which have actually happened." In other words, they see a linear continuity between commonsense or worldly realities and the actions of God. Luther rejects this linear thinking in favor of a theology of the cross. See also: linear and nonlinear thinking; Luther, Martin; theologian of the cross.

Theologian of the cross. Luther's term in the Heidelberg Disputation of 1518 for the theologian "who comprehends the visible and manifest things of God seen through suffering and the cross." The theologian of the cross understands the seeming paradox of God's weak power and foolish wisdom in 1 Corinthians 1. See also: linear and nonlinear thinking; Luther, Martin; theologian of glory.

Truth. Foucault by no means rejects the notion of truth, but understands it in a way that fits with his account of history and concepts. Truth, for Foucault, is "a thing of this world" which "is produced only by virtue of multiple forms of constraint." Different academic disciplines and cultural institutions (such as medicine and law) have different rules for producing truth in their respective domains, and these rules change over time. See also: anthropological universal; historical a priori.

Tuke, Samuel. 1784–1857. English Quaker and reformer whose Retreat for the insane near York is discussed by Foucault in *Discipline and Punish*, alongside the reforms of Philippe Pinel. Tuke's humane methods form, for Foucault, a regime of disciplinary power and normalization characteristic of the age of the asylum. See also: age of the asylum; Pinel, Philippe.

Velázquez, Diego. 1599–1660. Spanish painter whose canvas *Las Meninas* is treated in the opening chapter of Foucault's *The Order of Things*. Foucault argues that *Las Meninas* challenges conventions of representation (there is no single point of view from which all the lines of perspective make sense) and exposes the fragility of royal power, all of which places it on the cusp of the modern era. See also: modern era/episteme.

V-shaped dynamic. A term used in the present volume to describe the nonlinear account in Philippians 2 of Christ's self-emptying and subsequent exaltation by God. It contrasts with the linear account, according to which power is accrued incrementally and through steady progression. See also: linear and nonlinear thinking; x-shaped dynamic.

X-shaped dynamic. A term used in the present volume to describe the complex trajectories of 1 Corinthians 1. Those who humble themselves to seek wisdom and power at the cross will discover God's true wisdom and power (the "v" trajectory) and those who turn away from the cross will not discover the fullness of the power and wisdom for which they search (the "^" trajectory). Passing through the cross tears down and transfigures conceptions of power and wisdom. See also: linear and nonlinear thinking; v-shaped dynamic.

SELECT BIBLIOGRAPHY

Referenced Works by Foucault

There is no hermetic divide in Foucault scholarship between, on the one hand, his major book-length projects and, on the other, his interviews and lecture series at the Collège de France. This list is made up of the monographs and collections referenced in the current volume. I have supplied summaries of Foucault's major monographs, not because they are more important than the interviews and lectures, but because they are better known and are the texts which this volume has treated in greatest depth. The references are arranged by date of publication (first French edition/date of English translation).

(1961/1965/2006).[1] *History of Madness.* Translated by Jonathan Murphy and Jean Khalfa. London: Routledge, 2006. Charts the development of "madness" through medieval, Renaissance, Classical, and modern eras of Western thought in a way that prefigures Foucault's notion of epistemes in

---

1. The publishing of *Histoire de la folie* is explained in chapter 1, footnote 10.

Archaeology of Knowledge. Introduces elements of what he later came to call his archaeological method: history viewed as a series of ruptures, rather than a smooth continuity, with a focus on concepts rather than personalities. Foucault argues that the transition from Classical madhouses to modern asylums and psychoanalytic methods for the treatment of mental illness is not merely a humanitarian advance, but also the introduction of a new sort of control.

(1963/1973). *The Birth of the Clinic: An Archaeology of Medical Perception.* Translated by A. M. Sheridan-Smith. New York: Vintage Books, 1994. Foucault follows the transformation in the understanding of disease and the clinic in the move from the Classical to the modern age. In the Classical clinic, disease exists independently of its symptoms, whereas in the modern age the body is examined to reveal the severity of the disease infecting it. The modern clinic was born in an epistemological rupture at the end of the eighteenth century. Foucault coins the term "medical gaze" (*regard médical*) to designate the way in which a human person becomes an object, a body, in the medical context.

(1966/1970). *The Order of Things: An Archaeology of the Human Sciences.* London: Routledge, 2002. Analyzes the emergence of the human sciences across three distinct historical epistemes: Renaissance, Classical, and modern. While the Renaissance episteme constructs knowledge around resemblance and affinity, the Classical episteme privileges representation, and the modern episteme probes the limits of representation. The long book finishes with the famous claim, much misunderstood by casual readers of Foucault, that "man is an invention of recent date. And one perhaps nearing its end." *The Order of Things* became a best seller with wide general as well as scholarly appeal, entering the nonfiction best seller list of the magazine *L'Express* in April 1966.

(1969/2002). *The Archaeology of Knowledge and the Discourse on Language*. Translated by A. M. Sheridan-Smith. New York: Pantheon Books, 1971. Foucault's most theoretical work, *The Archaeology of Knowledge*, seeks to explain the archaeological method he made famous in *The Order of Things*. The notion of the episteme fades into the background (though it is still present), and Foucault focuses instead on discourse, discursive formations, and the archive. The book claims that Foucault's detractors "have probably found it difficult enough to recognize that their history, their economics, their social practices, the language that they speak, the mythology of their ancestors, even the stories that they were told in their childhood, are governed by rules that are not all given to their consciousness" (*AK*, 210–11). It never attained the popularity of *The Order of Things*.

(1975/1977). *Discipline and Punish*. Translated by A. M. Sheridan-Smith. New York: Vintage, 1995. The first of Foucault's two major genealogies, *Discipline and Punish* traces the history of "penal styles" from the Classical to the modern eras. The premodern penal regime was characterized by sovereign power (epitomized in the torture of Damiens, the attempted regicide), whereas modern penal practices privilege disciplinary power (characterized by Léon Faucher's rules "for the House of young prisoners in Paris"). Disciplinary power creates a disciplinary society, which seeks to observe and normalize the behavior of those living in it, creating docile bodies.

(1976/1978). *The History of Sexuality*. Vol. 1, *An Introduction* [published in French as *La volonté de savoir* (*The Will to Knowledge*)]. Translated by Robert Hurley. New York: Vintage, 1990. Foucault's second great genealogy, *The Will to Knowledge* charts the emergence of new categories of sexuality in the nineteenth century as a result of new biopolitical imperatives to monitor and control populations as a whole. Foucault repudiates the "repressive hypothesis," according to which the Victorians spoke little about sex, and he argues that we have misunderstood sexual "liberation." Finally, he asserts that the late twentieth-century West has become a "confessing society," throughout which the religious practice of confession has been transmuted and diffused.

(1977). *Language, Counter-Memory, Practice: Selected Essays and Interviews*. Ithaca, NY: Cornell University Press, 1977.

(1980). *Power/Knowledge: Selected Interviews and Other Writings, 1972–1977*. Edited by Colin Gordon. New York: Pantheon Books, 1980.

(1984). *The Foucault Reader*. Edited by Paul Rabinow. New York: Pantheon Books, 1984.

(1984/1985). *The History of Sexuality*. Vol. 2, *The Use of Pleasure*. Translated by Robert Hurley. New York: Random House, 1985. Foucault's first major "ethical" work, *The Use of Pleasure* is a study of sex in ancient Greece, through which he aims to address the question "Why is sexual conduct, why are the activities and pleasures that attach to it, an object of moral solicitude" in the modern era? (*HS2*, 10). Greek sexuality is studied in terms of "problematizations," or ways in which sex becomes a question and problem in ancient Greek culture. Ancient Greek sexuality, Foucault argues, is very different from the later Christian moralizing discourse on the flesh and prohibition.

(1984/1986). *The History of Sexuality*. Vol. 3, *The Care of the Self*. Translated by Robert Hurley. New York: Vintage, 1988. The third volume of Foucault's *History of Sexuality* addresses ancient Roman sexual attitudes and practices. Roman culture emerges as austere and suspicious of pleasure as an end in itself. Roman marriage is considered at length, as is the martial focus of Roman society. A great premium is put, in both Greek and Roman attitudes toward sex, on self-mastery and on what Foucault calls "the care of the self" (*le souci de soi*).

(1988). *Politics, Philosophy, Culture: Interviews and Other Writings, 1977–1984*. Edited by Lawrence D. Kritzman. New York: Routledge, 1988.

(1988). "Truth, Power, Self: An Interview with Michel Foucault." In *Technologies of the Self: A Seminar with Michel Foucault*, edited by Luther H. Martin, Huck Gutman, and Patrick H. Hutton, 9–15. Amherst, MA: University of Massachusetts Press, 1988.

(1989). *Foucault Live (Interviews, 1966–84)*. Edited by Sylvère Lotringer. New York: Semiotext(e), 1989.

(1991). "Politics and the Study of Discourse." In *The Foucault Effect: Studies in Governmentality: With Two Lectures by and an Interview with Michel Foucault*, edited by Graham Burchell, Colin Gordon, and Peter Miller, 53–62. Chicago: University of Chicago Press, 1991.

(1991). *Remarks on Marx: Conversations with Duccio Trombadori*. New York: Semiotext(e), 1991.

(1993). "About the Beginning of the Hermeneutics of the Self: Two Lectures at Dartmouth." *Political Theory* 21, no. 2 (1993): 198–227.

(1997). *The Essential Works of Foucault, 1954–1984*. Vol. 1, *Ethics: Subjectivity and Truth*. Edited by Paul Rabinow and James D. Faubion. New York: New Press, 1997.

(1997/2003). *Society Must Be Defended: Lectures at the Collège de France, 1975–76*. Edited by Mauro Bertani and Alessandro Fontana. New York: Picador, 2003.

(1998). *The Essential Works of Foucault, 1954–1984*. Vol. 2, *Aesthetics, Method, and Epistemology*. Edited by Paul Rabinow and James D. Faubion. New York: New Press, 1998.

(1988). "The Ethic of Care for the Self As a Practice of Freedom." In *The Final Foucault*, edited by James Bernauer and David Rasmussen, 1–20. Cambridge, MA: MIT Press, 1988.

(1999/2003). *Abnormal: Lectures at the Collège de France, 1974–1975*. Edited by Valerio Marchetti and Antonella Salomoni. New York: Picador, 2003.

(2000). *The Essential Works of Foucault, 1954–1984*. Vol. 3, *Power*. Edited by Paul Rabinow and James D. Faubion. New York: New Press, 2000.

(2003/2006). *Psychiatric Power: Lectures at the Collège de France, 1973–74*. Edited by Jacques Lagrange. Basingstoke: Palgrave Macmillan, 2006.

(2004/2007). *Security, Territory, Population: Lectures at the Collège de France, 1977–78*. Edited by Michel Senellart. Basingstoke: Palgrave Macmillan, 2007.

(2004/2008). *The Birth of Biopolitics: Lectures at the Collège de France, 1978–79*. Edited by Michel Senellart. Basingstoke: Palgrave Macmillan, 2008.

(2008/2011). *The Courage of Truth (The Government of Self and Others II): Lectures at the Collège de France, 1983–1984*. Edited by Frédéric Gros. Basingstoke: Palgrave Macmillan, 2011.

(2011). "The Gay Science." *Critical Inquiry* 37 (2011): 385–403.

(2011/2013). *Lectures on the Will to Know: Lectures at the Collège de France, 1970–1971, and Oedipal Knowledge*. Edited by Daniel Defert. New York: Palgrave Macmillan, 2013.

Other References, Including Works about Foucault

The secondary bibliography on Foucault is enormous. Here I restrict myself to books of two sorts: introductions liable to be useful and accessible to those discovering Foucault for the first time, and some of the most important books to discuss Foucault in relation to religious and theological themes. The list also includes full references for other works mentioned in this book.

Augustine of Hippo. *The City of God*. Harmondsworth: Penguin, 2004.

————. "The Teacher." In *Augustine: Earlier Writings*, edited by John H. S. Burleigh, 69–101. Philadelphia: Westminster Press, 1953.

Bachelard, Gaston. *The New Scientific Spirit*. Translated by Arthur Goldhammer. Boston: Beacon Press, 1984.

Bataille, Georges. *Eroticism: Death and Sensuality*. Translated by Mary Dalwood. San Francisco: City Lights, 1986.

Bernauer, James W. *Michel Foucault's Force of Flight: Toward an Ethics for Thought*. New York: Humanity Books, 2000. A powerful, scholarly treatment of Foucault, which draws out negative theological themes in Foucault's remorseless following through on the consequences of the death of God and his critique of humanism.

Brueggemann, Walter. *Genesis*. Atlanta: John Knox, 1982.

Caputo, John D. *The Weakness of God: A Theology of the Event*. Bloomington, IN: Indiana University Press, 2006.

Castelli, Elizabeth E. "Interpretations of Power in 1 Corinthians." *Semeia* 54 (1991): 197–222.

Cicero. "In Defense of Rabirius." In *The Speeches of Cicero*, translated by H. G. Lodge. London: Heinemann, 1927.

Coakley, Sarah. *Powers and Submissions: Spirituality, Philosophy and Gender*. Oxford: Blackwell, 2008.

Downing, Lisa. *The Cambridge Introduction to Michel Foucault*. Cambridge: Cambridge University Press, 2008. A well-written first introduction to the range of Foucault's thought, particularly suited to students of literature. Downing excels in her coverage of Foucault's engagement with Bataille, Blanchot, Klossowski, and Roussel, and in her refusal to synthesize or amalgamate Foucault's sometimes contradictory claims.

Carrette, Jeremy. *Foucault and Religion*. London: Routledge, 2002. Carrette seeks to read modern and contemporary culture in terms of a deterritorialized "religion," insisting that "it is necessary to find an interdisciplinary and historically located reading which seeks to appreciate the breadth and complexity of [Foucault's] work" (ix). Carrette highlights a religious question at the heart of Foucault's work.

———. *Religion and Culture: Michel Foucault*. London: Routledge, 2013.

Ehrensperger, Kathy. *Paul and the Dynamics of Power: Communication and Interaction in the Early Christ-Movement*. London: T&T Clark, 1997.

Frame, John. *The Doctrine of God*. Phillipsburg, NJ: P&R Publishing, 2002.

Fraser, Nancy. *Unruly Practices*. Cambridge: Polity Press, 1989.

Halperin, David M. *Saint Foucault: Towards a Gay Hagiography*. New York: Oxford University Press, 1995. Halperin explores Foucault's queer politics, which he brings into conversation with aspects of contemporary culture. Halperin seeks to defend Foucault against the critique that his account of sexuality as socially constructed is not "properly 'gay.'"

Hanby, Michael. *Augustine and Modernity*. London: Routledge, 2003.

Hegel, G. W. F. *Hegel's Philosophy of Nature*. Translated by A. V. Miller. Oxford: Oxford University Press, 2004.

———. *The Phenomenology of Mind*. Translated by J. B. Baillie. London: Routledge, 2015.

Helm, Paul. *The Providence of God*. Leicester: Inter-Varsity Press, 1994.

Lawlor, Leonard, and John Nale, eds. *The Cambridge Foucault Lexicon*. Cambridge: Cambridge University Press, 2014. A precious reference work for the student of Foucault. Over 700 pages of short articles (typically 3–4 pages) covering Foucault's major concepts, his influences, and interlocutors. Written by many of the leading names in Foucault scholarship, *The Cambridge Foucault Lexicon* is an excellent reference work to read alongside Foucault's own texts.

Lull, Timothy F., and William R. Russell, eds. *Martin Luther's Basic Theological Writings*. Minneapolis: Fortress Press, 2012.

Macey, David. *Michel Foucault*. London: Reaktion Books, 2004.

May, Todd. *The Philosophy of Foucault*. London: Routledge, 2014. A very well structured tour of Foucault's thought, framed by the question "Who are we?" May's volume serves, in parallel, as an introduction to Foucault and as an introduction to, and justification of, the study of philosophy.

Midelfort, Erik. "Madness and Civilization in Early Modern Europe: A Reappraisal of Michel Foucault." In *After the Reformation: Essays in Honour of J. H. Hexter*, edited by Barbara C. Malament, 247–66. Manchester: Manchester University Press, 1980.

Milbank, John. *Theology and Social Theory: Beyond Secular Reason*. 2nd ed. Oxford: Blackwell, 2006. Milbank's treatment of Foucault is brief and dismissive, but his account of power in Foucault is a symptom of his own thesis about the brute power that arises in the modern West and fails to capture some of the nuances of Foucault's position.

Miller, James. *The Passion of Michel Foucault*. New York: Simon and Schuster, 1993. A controversial biographical study of Foucault which seeks to connect his sexuality and sado-masochistic experiences on the one hand, and his writing on the other. Miller argues that Foucault's life and work can be understood in terms of an abiding fascination with death.

Mills, Sara. *Michel Foucault*. Routledge Critical Thinkers. London: Routledge, 2003. A good, accessible introduction to Foucault's main ideas and themes. Mills quotes Foucault liberally and interprets him lucidly: a good secondary book for the student new to Foucault.

Nietzsche, Friedrich. *"On the Genealogy of Morality" and Other Writings*. Edited by Keith Ansell-Pearson. Cambridge: Cambridge University Press, 2007.

Sartre, Jean-Paul. "Jean-Paul Sartre répond." *L'arc* 30 (1966): 87–97.

Schuld, J. Joyce. *Foucault and Augustine: Reconsidering Power and Love*. Notre Dame, IN: Notre Dame University Press, 2003. This thorough and generous reading of Foucault and Augustine explores their thought with a predisposition to find common areas of concern and common questions, only rarely overstating the case for their closeness. A very engaging demonstration of how Foucault might sensibly be brought into conversation with theology.

Smith, James K. A. *Who's Afraid of Postmodernism? Taking Derrida, Lyotard, and Foucault to Church*. Grand Rapids: Baker Academic, 2006.

Taylor, Charles. *A Secular Age*. Cambridge, MA: Harvard University Press, 2006.

Tran, Jonathan. *Foucault and Theology*. London: Bloomsbury, 2011. Tran helpfully engages with much of the secondary material on Foucault, giving the reader a sense of the main lines of Foucault criticism in relation to religion and theology. Perhaps a little too quick on occasion to read across between Foucault and the Bible, this book still provides an excellent overview of what is at stake between Foucault and theology.

Trueman, Carl R. *Luther on the Christian Life: Cross and Freedom*. Wheaton, IL: Crossway Books, 2015.

Van Til, Cornelius. *Christian Theistic Evidences*. Phillipsburg, NJ: Presbyterian and Reformed Publishing Company, 1978.

Verhey, Allen. *The Great Reversal: Ethics and the New Testament*. Grand Rapids: Eerdmans, 1984.

Watkin, Christopher. *Jacques Derrida*. Philipsburg, NJ: P&R Publishing, 2017.

———. *Thinking through Creation*. Philipsburg, NJ: P&R Publishing, 2017.

INDEX OF SCRIPTURE

INDEX OF SUBJECTS AND NAMES

Christopher Watkin (MPhil, PhD, Jesus College, Cambridge) researches and writes on modern and contemporary French thought, atheism, and religion. He works as senior lecturer in French studies at Monash University in Melbourne, Australia, where he lives with his wife, Alison, and son, Benjamin. His recent books include *Thinking through Creation: Genesis 1 & 2 as Tools of Cultural Critique* (2017), *French Philosophy Today: New Figures of the Human in Badiou, Meillassoux, Malabou, Serres and Latour* (2016), *Difficult Atheism: Post-Theological Thinking in Badiou, Meillassoux and Nancy* (2011), and *From Plato to Postmodernism: The Story of Western Culture through Philosophy, Literature and Art* (2011). He is also the author of *Jacques Derrida* (2017) in the P&R Great Thinkers series.

He blogs on French philosophy and the academic life at christopherwatkin.com and is a cofounder of audialteram partem.com, a site with the twin aims of bringing evangelical and Reformed theology into deep conversation with modern French philosophy and of encouraging scholars and scholarship working at the nexus of those traditions. You can find him on Twitter @DrChrisWatkin.

ALSO BY CHRISTOPHER WATKIN

With deftness and clarity, Christopher Watkin reclaims the Trinity and creation from their cultural despisers and shows how they speak into, question, and reorient some of today's most important debates.

"Watkin does much more than round up the usual proof texts: he rather calls our attention to biblical patterns that diagonally cut through taken-for-granted false dichotomies. . . . Take up and take heed."
> —**Kevin J. Vanhoozer**, Research Professor of Systematic Theology, Trinity Evangelical Divinity School

"Tears down false dichotomies in philosophy and lifts up treasures of truth. . . .This book helps us to inhabit biblical worlds of thought so that we can see, interpret, and reach our world with the gospel."
> —**Trevin Wax**, Bible and Reference Publisher, LifeWay Christian Resources

"Offers a radical and trenchant critique of contemporary culture and a well-grounded alternative shaped by the Christian Scriptures. I regard this slim volume as a seminal work, and I predict that it will become a classic of its kind."
> —**Albert M. Wolters**, Author, *Creation Regained*